Social Mobility Truths

Social Mobility Truths

Peter Saunders

CIVITAS

First Published
November 2019

© Civitas 2019

55 Tufton Street
London SW1P 3QL

email: books@civitas.org.uk

ISBN 978-1-912581-02-3

Typeset by Typetechnique

Printed in Great Britain
by 4edge Limited, Essex

Contents

Author

Peter Saunders is a sociologist who has written extensively on social class and inequality, poverty and welfare reform, and housing. He is a former Professor of Sociology at the University of Sussex (where he remains Professor Emeritus) and has held visiting positions at universities in the USA, Germany, Australia and New Zealand. He worked for ten years in Australia, first as Research Manager at the Australian Institute of Family Studies, and then as Research Director at the Sydney-based think tank, the Centre for Independent Studies, where he is a Distinguished Fellow. He is a Professorial Research Fellow at Civitas, with whom he has published reports on equalities policies, welfare reform and support for home ownership, as well as a series of reports on social mobility.

Acknowledgements

I am most grateful to Gary Marks and Robert Plomin for feedback and advice on an earlier draft. Gary Marks has also been enormously helpful in alerting me to new output in what is a rapidly-growing research area, as well as fielding repeated queries. Bruce Charlton and John Jerrim both helpfully responded at various times to inquiries about their work, and I continue to owe a debt of gratitude to Rod Bond, a former colleague at Sussex University, who was mainly responsible for developing the path model, reproduced here as Figure 3. Finally, thanks also go to David Green and his staff at Civitas who continue to offer an invaluable outlet for those who seek to challenge conventional wisdoms.

PART ONE
SOCIAL MOBILITY MYTHS

Social mobility and meritocracy

This year, 2019, marks the 75th anniversary of the 1944 *Education Act*. Often known as 'the Butler Act', after the Education Secretary of the time, R. A. Butler, this was the first explicit attempt by a British government to create a fully meritocratic system of education in which every child, regardless of their social background, would enjoy the opportunity to achieve their full potential.

Before the Second World War, state-aided grammar schools in England and Wales filled many of their places with fee-paying students (although applicants still had to pass an entrance examination). The law required that they offered a quarter of their places free of charge to bright children selected by a national Scholarship examination at age eleven, and over time the number of scholarship places expanded (by 1937, half of all grammar school places were being allocated in this way). Nevertheless, many bright children from poorer backgrounds still missed out.[1] Not only did this raise obvious issues of fairness, but it also led to a growing concern that the country was squandering vast pools of potential working class talent that it could not afford to lose.

The answer, addressed in the 1944 Act, was to make all state-aided secondary schools, including grammar schools, free for all pupils, irrespective of their social background or

---

[1] *The Education Act of 1944* www.parliament.uk/about/living-heritage/transformingsociety/livinglearning/school/overview/educationact1944/

their parents' financial means. A new national examination – the '11-plus' – was introduced, which tested for English, maths and general intelligence (IQ), and those scoring in the top quarter or third of marks were selected for grammar schools (the exact proportion depended on how many places were available in any given local authority area). Of the rest, children thought to have a technical bent were sent to new Technical schools, and everybody else went to 'Secondary Modern' schools, which offered a general education. In addition, the minimum age at which pupils were permitted to leave school was raised from fourteen to fifteen.

The 1944 Act was explicitly aimed at achieving equality of opportunity for children from different social class backgrounds. Because they would now recruit the brightest children from across the social spectrum, the grammar schools were re-cast as the conveyor belts of Britain's social class system, plucking talented youngsters from humble origins and propelling them into well-paid, high status, responsible positions in management and the professions.

Not everybody was happy with this. Some egalitarians in the Labour Party were less interested in equality of opportunity than equality of outcomes. They saw little difference in principle between selection on the basis of talent (the aim of the new system) or according to parental wealth and privilege, for both depended on the lottery of birth. Being born bright, like being born rich, was a matter of chance which individuals do nothing to 'deserve', so why should naturally talented children be singled out for special, fast-track treatment?

The best-known and most influential expression of this egalitarian critique came in Michael Young's dystopian novel, *The Rise of the Meritocracy*, published in 1958.[2]

---

[2] Michael Young, *The rise of the meritocracy* Thames and Hudson

Young foresaw a future in which a self-perpetuating elite of 'meritocrats,' selected for their cognitive ability, would dominate all the top positions in society. The members of this new elite would be insufferably smug, claiming they were entitled to their privileges because they had 'earned' (or 'merited') them in fair and open competition. And their children would tend to follow in their footsteps because they would often inherit their parents' talents and would therefore themselves qualify for places in the meritocratic elite. In Young's story, a demoralised and increasingly resentful cognitive underclass eventually rises up against this self-perpetuating elite and replaces the meritocracy with a more egalitarian system where everybody is treated the same, regardless of their natural abilities.

Our modern concept of meritocracy derives from Young's book. He famously defined 'merit' as 'ability plus effort', and a meritocracy as a system of ruling (or more generally, a system of recruitment) where all positions are allocated solely on the basis of individuals' intelligence and hard work. This remains its meaning today. But what's changed is the way we think about it.

Whereas Young regarded the growth of meritocracy as something to be avoided, later generations have embraced it as a desirable social policy objective. Nowadays, most politicians worry not that Britain is becoming too meritocratic, but that it is not meritocratic enough, and in the last twenty years, the pursuit of meritocracy has become the central feature of the social policy programmes of both Conservative and Labour governments.[3]

It is not just politicians who have come to regard

---

[3] Late in his life, Young despaired at the way his concept had been adopted and given a positive spin by the Blair Labour government. See Michael Young, 'Down with meritocracy' *The Guardian*, 29 June 2001

meritocracy in a more favourable light than Michael Young did. The great majority of the British public likewise see it as the fairest way of allocating positions and rewards. Public support for Young's egalitarian principle that everyone should be rewarded more-or-less equally, regardless of their talents, is quite limited (less than half the population think this is a good idea). But about nine out of ten Britons think it is fair to reward people according to their ability and how hard they work.[4]

Belief in the principle of meritocracy seems almost intuitive, a variant of the 'fairness/cheating instinct' identified in Jonathon Haidt's study of evolutionary psychology.[5] It seems obviously 'right' and 'fair' to most of us that those who work hardest should get the greatest rewards, and that those who perform best should take the lion's share of the proceeds. It's a gut feeling. The principle of meritocracy might not have appealed to Michael Young, but with 90 per cent support it's about as close as we are ever likely to come in this country to a consensus around a key principle of 'social justice.' No wonder politicians cleave to it.

The same meritocratic ideal that drove R. A. Butler and his fellow reformers 75 years ago, when they legislated to open up the grammar schools, therefore still drives our social policy thinking today. But this raises an obvious question. The Butler Education Act aimed to turn Britain into a

---

[4] In a 2011 survey, 85% of a UK representative sample agreed that 'In a fair society, people's incomes should depend on how hard they work and how talented they are', while only 41% agreed that, 'In a fair society, nobody should get an income a lot bigger or a lot smaller than anybody else gets' (Neil O'Brien, *Just Deserts?*, Policy Exchange, April 2011).

[5] Jonathon Haidt, *The Righteous Mind* (Pantheon Books, New York, 2012). Haidt points out that our instinctive regard for fairness can be tweaked in a left-wing or right-wing direction, so both egalitarianism and meritocracy may be felt to be fair: 'On the left, fairness often implies equality, but on the right it means proportionality – people should be rewarded in proportion to what they contribute, even if that guarantees unequal outcomes.' (p.138).

meritocracy by replacing grammar school fees with 'free' places allocated solely on the basis of talent, so how come, 75 years later, politicians of all parties are still pursuing this same outcome?

The answer is that many of our political leaders today believe that the competition for educational credentials and occupational success is still rigged, just as it was before the Second World War. They insist that children from middle class homes (those with parents in professional or managerial jobs) are still enjoying gross and unfair advantages over those from working class backgrounds (where parents work in more routine jobs in sectors like manufacturing or retailing). Indeed, many politicians think this situation has been getting *worse*.

If they are right, then modern Britain looks seriously flawed. Indeed, if 75 years of social democratic reforms really have failed to dent class privileges, it would be difficult to deny that much more radical changes may now be warranted.

Before he resigned in frustration at the lack of progress, the Chair of the government's Social Mobility Commission, Alan Milburn, came to precisely this conclusion. He said that if 'aspiration and ability' are to displace 'background or birth' as the main factors shaping people's lives in this country, then 'fundamental reforms' are needed, not just to the education system, but to the labour market, the housing market and the organisation of local economies. 'Tinkering with change,' he concluded, 'will not turn it around.'[6] A lot of people are starting to agree with him.

Before we buy into this radical agenda, however, it

---

[6] Government press release, 'Left behind Britain', 30 March 2017, www.gov.uk/government/news/left-behind-britain-narrowing-the-social-mobility-divide

would be wise to check on the facts. Milburn's assertion that background and birth still determine where people end up in life is widely shared among politicians and commentators in contemporary Britain, but there is a lot of evidence to suggest they are wrong. When we start to dig into the evidence on social mobility, it becomes clear that Britain is a lot more meritocratic than our political leaders seem to think it is. 'Background and birth' are not the key factors shaping our lives; 'aspiration and ability' are already the principal determinants of educational and occupational success.

The trouble is, very few people in positions of power and influence in this country have taken the trouble to familiarise themselves with this evidence. Public debate on social mobility in Britain has for the last twenty years been cloaked in a fog of myths and delusions, and this is now leading to some seriously misguided and in some cases damaging policies. It is time to clear the air.

Social mobility myths

In April this year the Social Mobility Commission issued its sixth *State of the Nation* report.[7] Much like the previous five, this latest report claimed there are major 'barriers' in Britain stopping working class children from succeeding in life, and that despite good intentions, government policies have done little to remove them. It complains that over the last four years, overall rates of social mobility in the UK haven't shifted at all, even though increasing social mobility has been a core commitment of both Labour and Conservative administrations ever since the early Blair years.

The Social Mobility and Child Poverty Commission (to give it its original title) was set up by Nick Clegg when he was Deputy Prime Minister in the Cameron Coalition government. Under the chairmanship of former Labour health minister Alan Milburn, it was given the task of monitoring social mobility in Britain and advising on ways of improving it. But after seven years in the job, during which time the social mobility rate hardly changed, Milburn resigned in December 2017, and his three fellow commissioners all resigned with him. Milburn wrote in his resignation letter: 'I have little hope of the current government making the progress I believe is necessary to bring about a fairer Britain.'[8]

---

[7] Social Mobility Commission, *State of the Nation 2018-19: Social mobility in Britain* HMSO, 2019

[8] Michael Savage, 'Theresa May faces new crisis after mass walkout over social policy' *The Guardian* 3 December 2017

Hoping to demonstrate its continuing commitment to 'fairness', Theresa May's government responded to Milburn's resignation by revamping the Commission. A new chair was appointed (Dame Martina Milburn – no relation to Alan), its annual budget was boosted by £2 million, and no fewer than twelve new commissioners – including a smattering of 'young people' and one or two minor celebs like the Editor of *Cosmopolitan* magazine – were drafted in to help her spend it. The reboot ticked every virtue-signalling box and exploited every politically-correct cliché. As the government press release earnestly explained: 'The twelve commissioners... are from diverse backgrounds, many with their own social mobility journeys... 3 commissioners are under 23 and are passionate about using their voice to help young people.'[9]

But the problem with the Social Mobility Commission never was its lack of diversity, youthful passion or commissioners on personal journeys. Its problem has always had more to do with its selective approach to evidence.

The tone was set from the very beginning. When the Commission launched in 2011, Milburn told listeners to the Radio 4 *Today* programme: 'We still live in a country where, invariably, if you're born poor you die poor.'[10] This rhetorical soundbite had absolutely no basis in fact (although it went unchallenged on air).

Milburn must have been familiar with research carried out for the Joseph Rowntree Foundation in 2006 which showed that *81 per cent* of children born to poor parents grow up to earn incomes above the poverty line.[11] What he

---

[9] 'SMC relaunch with 12 new commissioners and bigger research budget' Press release, www.gov.uk, 11 December 2018

[10] BBC Radio 4, *Today*, 5 April 2011

[11] Jo Blanden and Steve Gibbons. *The persistence of poverty across generations* Joseph Rowntree Foundation, 2006, Table 2.

should therefore have told Radio 4 listeners was that in this country, if you're born poor, you have a four in five chance of escaping poverty as an adult. This, however, would have clashed with the core assumptions to which Milburn and his Commission were already firmly wedded, even before they'd started work.

After I heard this broadcast, I tried to alert Milburn of his error, but I got no reply. Rather, he repeated his assertion in a subsequent report where he wrote of people 'being born poor and, *in all likelihood*, dying poor.'[12] It sounded so good, he used the line again – but it still wasn't true.

Following in her predecessor's footsteps, the new Commission chair, Dame Martina Milburn, was also interviewed on the *Today* programme on the day her first big report was published in 2019. Just like Alan Milburn, she could not resist the lure of hyperbole. 'It's very difficult,' she told the nation, 'for someone from a working class background to access professional jobs – even now.'[13]

Had Dame Martina read chapter one of her own report she would have discovered that 45 per cent of all the jobs in this country in 2018 were at professional or managerial level, and that no fewer than 34 per cent of the people doing them had been born into working class families.[14] It is true that people born to middle class parents are even more likely than those born to working class parents to end up in professional/managerial positions (60 per cent of them make it) – the key reasons for this continuing disparity will be explored in the following pages. But it clearly is not true that working class children find it 'very difficult' to get access to

---

[12] Alan Milburn, Foreword to *Fair Access to Professional Careers*, Cabinet Office, May 2012, p.7 (my emphasis)

[13] Interview on Radio Four Today programme, 30 April 2019

[14] Social Mobility Commission, *State of the Nation 2018-19: Social Mobility in Great Britain*, 2019 Figures 1.1 and 1.2

these jobs, for more than one-third of the people doing them were recruited from working class backgrounds.

These two Social Mobility Commission chairs, past and present, are not the only people guilty of exaggerating what they see as Britain's 'social mobility failure'. Almost all our leading politicians and social affairs journalists are signed up to the same discourse, regardless of whether they are socialists, liberals or conservatives.

In 2011, when he was Deputy Prime Minister with special responsibility for the government's social mobility strategy, Liberal Democrat leader Nick Clegg wrote: 'In Britain today, life chances are narrowed for too many by the circumstances of their birth... Patterns of inequality are imprinted from one generation to the next.'[15] But as we shall see (Truth #1, below), if we divide the population into three broad social classes, more than half of us end up in a different class from our parents (if we distinguish five classes, this proportion rises to 70 per cent) and this high level of fluidity shows no sign of reducing. Given these figures, it made absolutely no sense for Clegg to claim that inequalities are 'imprinted' by the 'circumstances of birth' from one generation to the next.

Conservative politicians are just as bad. When he was Education Secretary in 2012, Michael Gove declared: 'Those who are born poor are more likely to stay poor, and those who inherit privilege are more likely to pass on privilege, in England than in any comparable country. For those of us who believe in social justice, this stratification and segregation are morally indefensible.'[16] In the same year, Damian Hinds (who later succeeded Gove as Education Secretary in the May government) said: 'There are plenty of

[15] HM Government, *Opening Doors, Breaking Barriers: A strategy for social mobility*, April 2011, p.3
[16] Quoted in Greg Hurst, 'Domination by private schools is indefensible, declares Gove' *The Times* 11 May 2012

other countries that have much more mobility than us... the UK is almost always in the worst position.'[17] And in 2015, then Prime Minister David Cameron repeated: 'Britain has the lowest social mobility in the developed world... We cannot accept that.'[18] But these claims were all wrong. We shall see (Truth #5, below) that our rate of social mobility is around the average for advanced western countries, and is better than many. Claims that we are at the bottom of the pile are seriously methodologically flawed. We are not the international laggards we make ourselves out to be.

When Theresa May succeeded Cameron as Prime Minister, she kept up the same mantra. In a 2016 speech to youngsters in Derby she regretted that, 'For far too many children in Britain, the chance they have in life is determined by where they live or how much money their parents have.'[19] It must have been profoundly depressing for her young audience to hear the leader of their country tell them that their fate depends on ('*is determined by...*') where they happen to grow up and the size of their parents' bank accounts. If this were true, nobody could have blamed them for concluding that there is no point in working hard at school and striving to improve themselves, for their fates are already sealed. But it's not true. May's speech peddled a deeply-damaging and dispiriting falsehood.

Labour's spokesperson on social mobility, Jon Trickett, spins an equally miserable line. In a *Guardian* article in 2017, he wrote: 'As we approach the third decade of our new

---

[17] Launch of *7 Key Truths About Social Mobility*, Policy Exchange, 1 May 2012, available at: http://www.policyexchange.org.uk/events/past-events/item/seven-key-truths-about-social-mobility?category_id=37
[18] Quoted in Francis Green and David Kynaston, 'Britain's private school problem' *The Guardian* 13 January 2019
[19] Theresa May speech, 9 September 2016: *Britain: The great meritocracy* https://www.gov.uk/government/speeches/britain-the-great-meritocracy-prime-ministers-speech

century, it is still the case that the primary determinant of how well (or badly) you do in life is class, not your talent or effort.'[20] But it isn't! We shall see (Truths #14 and #15) that the impact of cognitive ability on educational and occupational outcomes is around *three times stronger* than the influence of class of origin. It's not class that is the 'primary determinant of how well or badly you do in life.' It's ability, or what Trickett called 'talent.' Labour's social mobility spokesperson is either unaware of these details, or just not interested.

Time and again, politicians of all parties tell us that social mobility in Britain is very low, that we perform much worse than other advanced western countries, that very few children from working class backgrounds succeed in landing good jobs, that the professions and our top universities are largely closed to people from humble origins, that opportunities for bright working class children are even worse today than they were in the past, and that very little has been achieved to remove the obstacles that stand in the way of children from lower class origins. As we shall see, *none* of this is true, yet it is nearly all uncritically accepted and routinely recycled by our social policy elites in Westminster and in the media. It must be having a devastating effect on the morale of our youngsters.

I have been studying social mobility in Britain, off and on, for the last 25 years. It has been a frustrating experience, for so often the claims made by those in a position to influence or determine public policy in this area are inaccurate, incomplete or both, and they seem uninterested in re-examining these myths when they are challenged. Social mobility in Britain has become a highly politicised topic,

---

[20] Jon Trickett, 'Social mobility isn't enough – a Labour government would tackle inequality' *The Guardian*, 1 December 2017.

and this has turned it into a matter of faith rather than fact. False claims have been repeated so many times that nobody even thinks of questioning them any more. The loss of face involved in acknowledging the truth would now be so huge that few politicians and commentators are likely to have the intellectual courage even to contemplate it. We have got locked into what one leading academic in this field calls a 'spiral of hyperbole.'[21]

It didn't use to be like this. Before the turn of this century, the study of social mobility was a specialist interest confined in Britain to a small number of academic sociologists. But after Tony Blair came to office and identified the pursuit of 'meritocracy' as a principal aim of his government, it mushroomed into a major research industry encompassing herds of economists, educationalists and psychologists as well as sociologists, and stretching out beyond academia into think tanks, quangos, the civil service, and the very heart of government.[22] A campaigning new think tank – the Sutton Trust – won the ear of government early on, a new quango – the Social Mobility Commission – began to direct much of the research by controlling the purse strings, and very soon a set of social mobility myths became so strongly entrenched in both government and the media that it became almost impossible to challenge them.

In 2010, driven by the naïve hope that I might correct some of the misleading claims which had taken root in public policy circles, I reviewed the evidence in a report called *Social Mobility Myths*, which was published by Civitas.

---

[21] John Goldthorpe, 'Understanding – and misunderstanding – social mobility in Britain' *Journal of Social Policy* vol.42, 2013, p.434

[22] Geoff Payne outlines the growth of this twenty-first century 'social mobility industry' in his book, *The new social mobility* (Policy Press, 2017), chapter 3. He estimates that media coverage of social mobility issues has increased ten-fold as a result.

It demonstrated that most politicians are misguided in their beliefs regarding social mobility in this country, and that a lot of damage was being done (and money being wasted) in trying to rectify problems that either did not exist, or were a lot less daunting than claimed. I hoped that publishing this critique through a public policy think-tank, rather than in some obscure academic journal, would help bring the material to the attention of policy makers and journalists. But while it did stir some short-term media interest, the book had no impact at all on the people in charge of the policies.

Two years later, I tried again, this time with a shorter Civitas report entitled *Social Mobility Delusions*. This second report updated the earlier material, corrected some influential yet flawed new arguments that had emerged since the first report was published, and speculated on why the powers-that-be are so reluctant to accept that Britain is a much more open society than they think it is. But this second attempt at shifting the terms of the debate achieved no more impact than the first one had.

Both of these reports are still available online and can be downloaded from the Civitas website free of charge.[23] In this third bite at the cherry I have included key evidence from both of them, updated it with the latest social mobility research findings, and introduced some completely new material based on exciting new research in behavioural genetics which helps us understand what really influences children's educational and occupational achievements as they grow up (it was reading Robert Plomin's *Blueprint*, a summary of recent work on the importance of genes for human behaviour, that finally prompted me to return to this issue).[24]

---

[23] Peter Saunders, *Social Mobility Myths* (Civitas, 2010): http://www.civitas.org.uk/pdf/SocialMobilityJUNE2010.pdf; Peter Saunders, *Social Mobility Delusions* (Civitas 2012): http://www.civitas.org.uk/pdf/socialmobilitydelusions2012.pdf

[24] Robert Plomin, *Blueprint: How DNA makes us who we are*, Allen Lane, 2018

Inevitably, this essay will touch on some detailed and complex material, but I have tried to write it in an accessible style, so that even politicians should be able to follow it. I have avoided using tables, graphs and algebraic equations wherever possible (if you want this stuff, you can find a lot of it in my earlier publications or by following up the citations in the footnotes). Instead, I have organised the evidence into a series of simple statements which I call 'social mobility truths.' I contrast these truths with the myths and delusions that still litter so much of our public debate.

I am well aware that social scientists generally shy away from using words like 'truth' and 'fact', for evidence is always fallible, knowledge is always partial and incomplete, and claims to truth are (or should be) always vulnerable to future refutation. But the claims I shall be making are all based on empirical evidence which is publicly available and can be tested. These are not my opinions; they are statements based on facts. That is why I refer to them as 'truths.' I have identified twenty-four of them.

It would be nice to think that politicians might take the time to pay these truths some serious attention. But given past experience, I'm not holding my breath.

Social mobility: Definitions and measurement

Social mobility refers to the movement of individuals from one socio-economic position to another. It may occur upwards or downwards (i.e. people may improve their situation, or it may deteriorate), but when politicians talk about 'increasing social mobility' they nearly always focus only on upward movement.

Social mobility may be measured over the course of people's lives, comparing their position when they first enter the labour market with their eventual destination ('intra-generational mobility'), or it may be measured by comparing the situations of parents and their children at roughly the same ages ('inter-generational mobility'). Most policy discussion relates to inter-generational mobility.

Socio-economic positions can be conceptualised and measured in various different ways, but generally, sociologists look at movement between 'social classes' (based on occupational categories) or up and down occupational status hierarchies, while economists are more interested in movement between different income groups (usually, earnings quartiles). Social mobility is also sometimes measured on an educational dimension (e.g. comparing years of education, or qualifications achieved, by parents and their children).

Social classes are distinguished according to people's relationship to the labour market – whether they are employed, employers or self-employed, and (if employed) how much control and autonomy they exercise in their work and how much financial benefit and security they gain from it. In this report we focus mainly on the distinction between 'middle class' jobs (mainly professional or managerial employment, corresponding to Classes 1 and 2 in the National Statistics system of classification) and 'working class' jobs (semi-routine or routine occupations such as drivers, machinists, sales assistants and cleaners, corresponding to Classes 6 and 7). Positions between these two are designated as 'intermediate' classes.

Social mobility rates may be estimated in absolute terms (the proportion of individuals born into one social class who end up in another), or in relative terms (the chances of individuals from different social class origins ending up in different class destinations). Public debate has often confused the two.

If the number of middle class jobs expands over time, and the size of the working class contracts, absolute mobility rates will rise, but this does not necessarily mean that the relative chances of middle class and working class children ending up in middle class or working class jobs has changed. Changes in absolute mobility rates do not therefore necessarily indicate changes in social fluidity.

PART TWO
SOCIAL MOBILITY TRUTHS

Truth #1

Social mobility in Britain is widespread

Although you'd never know it listening to our politicians, there is extensive social mobility in Britain, and we have known about this for at least forty years.

It was back in 1980 when Oxford sociology professor, John Goldthorpe, surprised himself and most of his profession by publishing results from a survey of ten thousand British men which showed that social mobility was much more common than had hitherto been realised or acknowledged.[25] Dividing his respondents into three broad classes (professional/managerial people at the top, semi- and unskilled workers at the bottom, and an intermediate class in between), Goldthorpe found that 49 per cent of them were occupying a different class position from that of their fathers at a similar age.[26]

---

[25] Up until then, sociologists had been relying on an extremely unreliable study conducted in the late 1940s by David Glass which had wrongly claimed that mobility is very limited in scope and range. I discuss this earlier study, and its weaknesses, in chapter 1 of *Social Mobility Myths*. Note that Goldthorpe's research was limited to men because, in the period he was looking at, men were generally the dominant wage earners in most households, many women did not have paid employment, and those that did were often only in part-time jobs. Most women's 'class situations' were thus dictated by what their husbands did for a living. More recent mobility studies have included women as well as men, reflecting the large increase that has occurred in female labour force participation.

[26] John Goldthorpe, *Social Mobility and Class Structure in Modern Britain* (Clarendon Press, Oxford, 1980). For the remainder of this report, I will refer to people in professional and managerial occupations as 'middle class', and those in routine

While 57 per cent of the men who had been born to 'working class' fathers (defined as people employed in non-supervisory manual work) had remained in the working class, 27 per cent had risen to 'intermediate' class positions (e.g. technicians, supervisors, white-collar workers and small business people), and 16 per cent had made it to what Goldthorpe called 'the salariat' or the 'service class' (defined as professionals, managers and higher-level administrators who are paid a salary for their services, as well as owners of large businesses).[27] Similarly, while 59 per cent of those born into the professional-managerial class had managed to stay there, 26 per cent had fallen into the intermediate class, and 15 per cent had dropped into the working class.

Later research not only confirmed Goldthorpe's finding of extensive social mobility, but found even more movement across social classes than he reported. His research was carried out in 1972, which meant most of the men in his sample were born before the Second World War, and many of their fathers were born before the First World War. It is in the nature of social mobility research that we are always looking backwards in time, and Goldthorpe's study was mainly reporting on inter-generational mobility patterns from the first half of the twentieth century. Later studies covering younger generational cohorts have revealed that social mobility has become even more widespread since then.

---

and semi-routine jobs as 'working class.' The former correspond to Classes 1 and 2 in the *National Statistics Socio-Economic Classification* (Office for National Statistics, Palgrave Macmillan, 2005) and the latter to classes 6 and 7 (jobs like factory machinists, drivers, fitters, office receptionists, kitchen staff, porters and cleaners). Classes 3, 4 and 5 (covering ancillary administrative staff, the self-employed, and lower-level technical and supervisory jobs are referred to as 'intermediate classes'.

[27] Goldthorpe uses the term 'service class' because these people render a professional or management 'service' to employers or clients. However, it is a potentially confusing term with connotations of 'being in service' or 'servility'. In this essay, therefore, I use the terms 'middle class' or 'professional-managerial class' to identify this stratum.

Just a decade later, for example, Goldthorpe himself reported on some 1983 survey data which showed that 53 per cent of men then in employment had changed classes compared with their fathers. The proportion of working class sons entering the professional-managerial class was now up from 16 to 22 per cent, and the proportion remaining where they were had fallen from 57 to 47 per cent.[28] A national survey carried out at around the same time by Gordon Marshall and others similarly confirmed that one-third of all men and women in the professional-managerial class in the mid-1980s had started life in the manual working class.[29]

From the 1990s onwards, researchers have been able to measure inter-generational social mobility rates by following the progress of members of various birth cohorts. Repeated surveys of thousands of people born in one week in 1958, and then again of people born in one week in 1970, both show extensive mobility up and down the class structure once these individuals achieved adulthood. By 1991, for example, when they reached age 33, 45 per cent of the men and 39 per cent of the women in the 1958 birth cohort had moved upwards relative to the social class of their parents, and 27 per cent of the men and 37 per cent of the women had moved down. For the 1970 cohort (assessed in 2000 at age 30), the equivalent figures were 42 per cent (men) and 41 per cent (women) moving up, and 30 per cent (men) and 35 per cent (women) moving down.[30]

An even more recent sample of men and women born between 1980 and 1984, taken from the first wave of the

---

[28] John Goldthorpe, *Social Mobility and Class Structure in Modern Britain* (second edition, Clarendon Press, Oxford, 1987). All future references are to this second edition.

[29] Gordon Marshall, Howard Newby, David Rose and Carolyn Vogler, *Social Class in Modern Britain* (London, Hutchinson, 1988).

[30] John Goldthorpe and Michelle Jackson, 'Intergenerational class mobility in contemporary Britain' *British Journal of Sociology* vol.58, 2007, 525-46.

UK Household Longitudinal Study, has reported similar findings. Most of these people were still under 30 years of age at the time of the research, and we know that considerable mobility continues to occur beyond this age.[31] Nevertheless, looking at their mobility across 7 social classes (an expanded version of the more familiar 3 class model), more than three-quarters of the men and about 80 per cent of the women were already occupying a different class from that of their parents. The authors report that this level of mobility is 'highly consistent' with overall mobility rates measured across 7 classes for cohorts born in 1946, 1958 and 1970.[32]

Another analysis of the UK Household Longitudinal Study has compared social mobility rates for cohorts born in the 1950s and 1960s with those born between 1975 and 1981. Measuring movement between 5 social classes, it reports that, 'The rate of total mobility remains more or less stable at approximately 70 per cent for both men and women across the three cohort groups.'[33]

All these studies agree that it is more unusual today for somebody to stay in the social class in which they were born than to move out of it, either up or down. This is confirmed by the Social Mobility Commission's *State of the Nation* 2019 report, which analyses the class composition of the 2018 UK workforce based on the Office of National Statistics' Labour Force Survey.

---

[31] Erzsebet Bukodi et al, 'The mobility problem in Britain; New findings from the analysis of cohort data' *British Journal of Sociology*, vol.66, 2015, pp.93-117. The Household Longitudinal Study is based on the decennial census of England and Wales and links 1% of the population from 1971, through 1981, 1991 and 2001, to 2011.

[32] Bukodi et al, 'The mobility problem in Britain' p.102.

[33] Franz Buscha and Patrick Sturgis, 'Declining social mobility? Evidence from five linked censuses in England and Wales 1971-2011' *British Journal of Sociology*, vol.69, 2018, p.166

It finds that 65 per cent of people born to working class (defined as semi-routine and routine worker) parents have been upwardly mobile, and 40 per cent of those born to professional-managerial parents have been downwardly mobile. One-third (34%) of those starting out in the working class now find themselves in professional-managerial positions.[34]

This does not look like a static, rigid, closed society; it looks more like a remarkably fluid and open one. Social mobility is the norm in Britain, not the exception, and it covers the range from top to bottom. This has been the case for at least fifty years, although you'd never know it listening to our politicians.

---

[34] The *State of the Nation* report actually finds that 40% of those born to professional/managerial parents are downwardly mobile, 16% of them falling all the way to the working class. This is a bit higher than the figures reported in earlier studies. We shall see later that absolute rates of male downward mobility in Britain have been rising, while absolute rates of male upward mobility have been falling – an outcome which reflects the larger number of people born to middle class parents (and smaller number born to working class parents) now than in the past, due to the twentieth century expansion in the size of the middle class.

Truth #2

The present generation has at least as good a chance of getting a middle class job as any previous generation enjoyed

We are often told by journalists and politicians that young people today are the first generation to face worse career prospects than their parents. The Social Mobility Commission's Chair and Deputy Chair introduced the Commission's 2017 *State of the Nation* report, for example, by stating: 'Britain's deep social mobility problem, for this generation of young people in particular, is getting worse not better.'[35] But statements like this are misleading, for they rest on a misunderstanding of what the evidence is telling us.

Through most of the twentieth century, the growth of public sector employment, coupled with technological and economic innovation, resulted in a substantial expansion in the size of the professional-managerial class (and a corresponding contraction in the size of the manual working class). As recently as 1951, more than half the working population of Britain was still employed in routine or semi-routine working class occupations – jobs like labouring, cleaning, driving or factory work – and only one in ten were in professional or managerial occupations (the so-called 'middle class'). Today, the size of the middle class has

---

[35] Social Mobility Commission, *State of the Nation 2017: Social Mobility in Britain* (HMSO, 2017), p.iii

quadrupled to around 40 per cent, and the working class has dwindled to less than one-third of the workforce.[36]

This huge expansion in the number of professional and managerial positions resulted in a high *absolute* rate of upward social mobility in all developed countries, including Britain, during much of the twentieth century. In each generation, there were more 'top jobs' to fill, so increasing numbers of people born into lower class positions had to be recruited in order to fill them.

This change benefited everybody. Children born into the working class now had more opportunity than their parents had enjoyed to clamber into middle class jobs, but children born into the middle class also now found that their chances of staying in that class had improved to a similar extent.

Clearly, this expansion of the middle class could not go on for ever. The more the number of professional and managerial positions grew, the less scope there was for further expansion in the next generation. Eventually, there had to come a saturation point, for we cannot all be middle class.[37] For men, it seems that we reached this point about twenty years ago. Ever since then, the expansion of male, middle class jobs has slowed or even halted, and this is reflected in a levelling-off, and perhaps even a fall, in absolute rates of upward mobility of men. For women, the

---

[36] Trevor Noble, 'The mobility transition' *Sociology* vol.34, 2000; Erzsebet Bukodi and John Goldthorpe, *Social mobility and education in Britain* (Cambridge University Press, 2019, p.35).

[37] Goldthorpe argues that there is still some scope for further expansion by what he calls 'upgrading the class structure' (Erzsébet Bukodi and John Goldthorpe, *Social mobility and education in Britain*, Cambridge University Press, 2019, p.214). This means replacing routine jobs with jobs offering higher pay, more job security and better career prospects. The fact remains, however, that there are inherent limits. It is difficult to imagine any economy where everybody is a manager or a professional and nobody is paid to clean streets or wipe down tables.

expansion is still continuing, although this too must stop at some point.[38]

Buscha and Sturgis use the Household Longitudinal Survey to compare the social mobility experiences of men and women born in 1955-61 with those born two decades later.[39] They report that, by the time the men reached their early-mid thirties, downward mobility had increased slightly (from 28 per cent in the earlier cohort to 30 per cent in the later one) and upward mobility had reduced slightly (from 40 to 38 per cent). For women, however, upward mobility was still increasing (up from 34 to 39 per cent) while downward mobility was still falling (35 to 29 per cent).

As male upward mobility rates have started to reduce, downward mobility rates have started increasing, leaving the overall male fluidity rate unchanged. In their analysis of the experience of four different British birth cohorts (1946, 1958, 1970, and 1980-84), Erzsébet Bukodi and her colleagues estimate that men in the earliest cohort were about 3 times more likely to experience upward rather than downward movement, but those in the most recent cohort are more-or-less evenly split between upward and downward movers.[40]

On the face of it, this sounds like bad news (at least for men), but given the changes which have taken place in the relative sizes of the middle class and working class, we should not be surprised by these patterns. The proportion of children born into professional-managerial households tripled between the 1946 and 1980-84 cohorts, and this has vastly increased the size of the pool from which downward

---

[38] Yaojun Li and Fiona Devine, 'Is social mobility really declining?' *Sociological Research Online* vol.16, 2011. Li and Devine report that male absolute mobility rates were unchanged overall between 1991 and 2005, but downward mobility increased while upward mobility decreased. For women, there was no change.

[39] Franz Buscha and Patrick Sturgis, 'Declining social mobility?', op cit.

[40] Bukodi et al, 'The mobility problem in Britain' op cit.

mobility can now occur. Similarly, the proportion of people born into working class households halved between the oldest and the youngest of these cohorts, which means there is now a much smaller pool of working class individuals available to achieve upward mobility.

Of the 1946 cohort of men, 53 per cent were born to working class parents and just 14 per cent to professional/ managerial parents, but 26 per cent were middle class by the age of 27 (36 per cent by their mid-thirties), with just 35 per cent ending up in the working class (32 per cent by their mid-thirties). Compare this with the early eighties cohort, where only 26 per cent were born to working class parents (half the number forty years earlier) while 37 per cent (two and a half times as many) started life in the professional-managerial middle class. By their mid-twenties, 38 per cent had middle class jobs and 32 per cent were in working class occupations (it is currently too early to know their class destinations by their mid-late thirties).

In short, experience of upward mobility is becoming less common *because so many of us are already middle class.* Many politicians and researchers seem to have misunderstood or misinterpreted this. Three points, in particular, are crucial.

First, the fact that the expansion of the middle class is slowing (and for men seems to have stopped) does not mean that *overall* mobility rates are falling, still less that British society is becoming 'more closed' or 'less fair.' Just as many people are changing class as ever before – social mobility is not 'grinding to a halt.' The difference now is that more people are dropping downwards, and fewer are rising upwards, than used to be the case, and the reason for this is that there are now more people in positions from which it is possible to fall, and fewer in positions from which it is possible to rise. Politicians who worry that social mobility as a whole is declining are mistaken (those who want upward mobility to keep rising with no corresponding increase in downward mobility are only fooling themselves).[41]

Secondly, the slow-down in upward mobility, and increase in downward mobility, does not mean that children today have less chance than their parents did to gain middle class employment. The middle class is at least as large for them as it was for their parents, and it will remain so, so their chance of getting a middle class job is just as great. It is absurd to complain, as the Social Mobility Commission has done, that a decline in absolute upward mobility means prospects for young people have worsened. The statistical likelihood of their experiencing upward mobility is lower, but this is only because so many of them are already in the middle class.[42]

Thirdly, it makes no sense to argue, as so many politicians do, that we can return to earlier levels of upward mobility by boosting education and training. Paper qualifications help individuals compete more successfully for middle class jobs, but increasing the number of people with paper qualifications does nothing to expand the number of middle class positions available for them to fill.[43] As John Goldthorpe

---

[41] John Goldthorpe cites the example of Tony Blair's determination in the early years of this century to get social mobility increasing 'as it did in the decades after the war' ('Understanding – and misunderstanding – social mobility in Britain', op cit., p.437). As Goldthorpe points out, it is not the social mobility rate that has changed, but the structure of the job market, and Blair would almost certainly have resisted any attempt to increase downward mobility in order to make more room available at the top.

[42] This is not to deny that levels of dissatisfaction may start to rise as more people experience downward mobility and fewer experience upward mobility. Now that the middle class is so large, falling out of it may provoke a sense of 'relative deprivation' much stronger than that associated in earlier periods with a failure to get into it – even though the chance of getting a middle class job is as good as it has ever been. I discussed this relative deprivation problem in the appendix to *Social Mobility Myths*.

[43] Geoff Payne, 'Labouring under a misapprehension: Politicians' perceptions and the realities of structural social mobility in Britain 1995-2010' In Paul Lambert et al., *Social Stratification: Trends and Processes*, Aldershot, Ashgate, 2012.

patiently explains, 'Education has an effect on *who* is mobile, or immobile, rather than on the overall rate of mobility.'[44]

The Social Mobility Commission has predicted 'a social mobility dividend for our country' if we keep increasing the supply of highly-qualified people.[45] This is nonsense. What governs the absolute rate of upward social mobility is not the supply of skilled labour, but demand from employers. The proportion of young people with degrees is already higher in Britain than in most other OECD countries, yet thousands of them are finding there are not enough graduate-level jobs to absorb them – only 52 per cent of recent graduates are in jobs that require a degree.[46] Giving youngsters more qualifications will not increase upward mobility nor expand the size of the middle class.

---

[44] Goldthorpe 'Understanding – and misunderstanding – social mobility in Britain', op cit., p.441

[45] Social Mobility Commission, *Fair Access to Professional Careers*, op cit., p.1

[46] Chartered Institute of Personnel and development Policy Report, *The graduate employment gap: expectations versus reality* November 2017, p.3

Truth #3

Middle class children are between 2 and 3 times more likely to end up in middle class jobs than working class children

So far we have been looking at the absolute rate of social mobility where we have seen that movement of individuals between the working class and middle class, down as well as up, is widespread. However, the question which goes to the heart of the fairness of British society is whether people born into different social classes enjoy equal social mobility chances.

Here, there is no dispute that children born to professional-managerial parents are more likely to get middle class jobs when they grow up than are children born to working class parents. Similarly, they are less likely to end up in working class jobs. It is this difference in *relative* mobility chances which is at the centre of the meritocracy debate in this country.

In his pioneering 1972 survey, John Goldthorpe measured relative social mobility chances by means of two statistics: *disparity ratios* and *odds ratios*. A disparity ratio expresses the relative likelihood of children from different social class origins arriving at the same social class destination. For example, if 20 per cent of those from working class backgrounds achieve middle class positions, and 60 per cent of those from middle class backgrounds achieve middle class positions, there is a 3:1 disparity in the relative chances of occupational success enjoyed by middle class as compared with working class children.

An odds ratio calculates the chances of a child from a higher class position falling to a lower class or remaining where they are, and compares this with the chances of a child from the lower class rising to the higher class or remaining where they are. This results in a summary statistic which can be used to compare overall fluidity rates over time, or across countries.[47]

Goldthorpe reasoned that, if people's class origins played no part in shaping their destinations, all disparity ratios (and therefore odds ratios too) should be 1:1. A working class child should be just as likely as a middle class child to end up as a doctor or an accountant, and a middle class child should be just as likely as a working class child to end up as a shop assistant or factory operative. What he found back in the early seventies, however, was a disparity ratio of nearly 4:1, when comparing the chances of children who had been born to professional-managerial class fathers and those born to working class fathers each achieving a middle class position in adulthood. A similar ratio of about 4:1 was also recorded when comparing the chances of a working class and middle class child ending up in a working class job.

By comparing different birth cohorts within his sample, Goldthorpe demonstrated that these ratios had remained fairly constant over much of the twentieth century. However, in his follow-up analysis using data from a 1983 survey he

---

[47] The formula to calculate an odds ratio summarising overall fluidity between two classes, a and b, is

$(F_{aa}/F_{ab}) \div (F_{ba}/F_{bb})$

where F_{aa} is the number of people from class a ending up in class a; F_{ab} is the number from class a who end up in class b; F_{ba} is the number from class b ending up in class a; and F_{bb} is the number from class b who remain in class b. See Bukodi and Goldthorpe, *Social mobility and education in Britain*, p.53.

found that the disparity in the chances of middle class and working class children achieving a middle class destination had fallen during the previous decade from around 4:1 to around 3:1, while the disparity in their chances of ending up in a working class position had increased to almost 5:1.[48] The chances against working class success had therefore reduced somewhat, while those against middle class failure had lengthened.

Different researchers define and draw boundary lines between social classes in slightly different ways, and this will obviously affect the proportions of people they identify moving from one class location to another. Nevertheless, other studies since Goldthorpe have all found substantial disparities in the class destinations of those born into working class or middle class homes, no matter how these classes are identified. Most of these later studies nevertheless report disparities lower than his initial 4:1.

Heath and Payne used data collected in election surveys in the last third of the twentieth century to estimate that, on average, individuals from professional-managerial families were 3.3 times more likely than those from working class families to end up in middle class jobs, and were 3.5 times less likely to end up in working class jobs.[49] Analysis of data from the two national birth cohort studies which have followed thousands of individuals born in 1958 and 1970 also generates disparity ratios in the order of 3:1 by the time cohort members reached their thirties.[50]

---

[48] The 1983 survey results are reported in the second edition of Goldthorpe's book, in chapter 9, which is co-authored with Clive Payne. Note that while the two disparity ratios changed, the odds ratio stayed more-or-less the same.

[49] Anthony Heath and Clive Payne, 'Twentieth Century Trends in Social Mobility in Britain' Centre for Research into Elections and Social Trends *Working Paper* No.70, June 1999, University of Oxford

[50] See *Social Mobility Myths*, Table 3

The most recent estimates of relative mobility rates we have come from the Social Mobility Commission, which draws on data from the Labour Force Survey. Its 2019 report suggests that individuals born into the working class are just over twice as likely as those from the middle class to end up in working class jobs, and that those born to middle class parents are almost twice as likely to end up in middle class jobs.[51]

People from middle class origins therefore continue to out-compete those from working class origins – both in the contest for middle class jobs, and in avoiding working class destinations – although the gap between them appears to have been narrowing somewhat.

---

[51] 16% of professional-managerial class people end up in working class jobs compared with 35% of working class people – a disparity ratio of just over 2:1. 34% of people from working class backgrounds end up in the professional-managerial class compared with 60% of those from professional-managerial backgrounds – a disparity ratio of under 2:1. Social Mobility Commission, *State of the Nation 2018-19*, op cit., pp.3-4

Truth #4

There has been no reduction in social mobility between classes over recent decades

The growth in size of the middle class is now slowing, which means the huge scale of upward mobility witnessed in the past is unlikely to be repeated in the future. But this does not mean that British society is becoming any less open. To assess this, we need to track overall fluidity over time (i.e. changes in the likelihood that people who are born into different classes will arrive at different or similar class destinations). We can do this by using odds ratios.

Evidence from several different studies drawing on different samples confirms that, even though the total amount of upward mobility for men is now less than it used to be, the total amount of 'relative class mobility' measured by odds ratios (i.e. the probability of a working class child getting into the middle class rather than staying put, and of a middle class child ending up in the working class rather than staying put) has not reduced. Indeed, it has almost certainly risen somewhat since the 1950s.

Heath and Payne's analysis of odds ratios calculated from election survey data (where voters' class origins and current class were both collected) found the probability of working class boys ending up in middle class jobs, and of middle class boys ending up in working class jobs, increased in the second half of the twentieth century, although there was no significant change for girls.[52] This was confirmed by Gershuny's analysis of mobility patterns in the British Household Panel Study (a random sample of the British population who are re-visited each year). Looking at people's occupations by the time they reached 35 years of age, he found consistently falling odds ratios (based on professional-managerial class/working class comparisons) for successive generations born after 1940.[53]

Comparison of the 1991 British Household Panel Survey and the 2005 General Household Survey by Li and Devine similarly reports 'a slight but significant increase in fluidity' over this period.[54] A review by Goldthorpe and Mills of thirteen different surveys carried out between 1972 and 2005 also finds 'some possible indication of a...trend towards increasing fluidity', and nothing to support the idea that relative mobility has been declining.[55]

Goldthorpe's most recent book, with Bukodi, concludes that there has been little change (perhaps a slight increase) in fluidity for men (comparing the 1958 and 1970 birth cohorts), but a definite increase in fluidity for women. The latter, however, is mainly due to downward mobility among middle class women who choose after starting a family to combine child-rearing with less demanding, part-time work.[56]

---

[52] Adrian Heath and Clive Payne, 'Twentieth century trends in social mobility in Britain', op cit. In various general election surveys respondents were asked for their own, and their parents', occupations, from which it is possible to measure social mobility rates.

[53] Jonathon Gershuny, 'Beating the odds (1): Inter-generational social mobility from a human capital perspective' University of Essex, Institute for Social & Economic Research *Working papers* No.17, 2002

[54] Yaojun Li and Fiona Devine, 'Is social mobility really declining?' op cit, para 5.3

[55] John Goldthorpe and Colin Mills, 'Trends in inter-generational class mobility in modern Britain' *National Institute Economic Review*, 2008, p.93. The review included both the 1958 and 1970 birth cohort studies, as well as research based on the General Household Survey, the EU Income and Living Conditions Survey, and election surveys.

[56] Bukodi and Goldthorpe, *Social Mobility and Education in Britain*, chapter 3.

Perhaps the most authoritative analysis is by Buscha and Sturgis who use the Household Longitudinal Survey (based on the decennial national census) to compare relative mobility rates for men and women born in the late fifties, late sixties and late seventies by the time they reached age 30-36. They found that the association between class of origin and class of destination weakened significantly between the first two cohorts, and remained at this lower level for the third cohort. For men and for women, the strength of the association in the first and second cohorts fell by around 17 per cent, meaning that it became less possible to predict somebody's social class from the class of their parents. Put another way, relative mobility chances increased between the late 1980s (when the first cohort reached its thirties) and the late 1990s (when the second cohort reached this age), and then stayed at this level through to the first decade of this century (when the third cohort reached this age).[57]

Politicians rarely if ever refer to any of this work.

Instead, they rely overwhelmingly on one study by a group of economists working on behalf of the Sutton Trust who claim that *income mobility* (or more accurately, earnings mobility, for they only look at people in paid employment) has been falling. They base this claim on a comparison of estimated parental and children's earnings in the 1958 and 1970 birth cohort studies. Finding a stronger statistical association in the later study, they conclude that social fluidity declined substantially in the space of little over a decade.[58]

---

[57] Buscha and Sturgis, 'Declining social mobility?' op cit. The pattern for women is slightly more complicated than for men in that they show the same increase in fluidity between the first 2 cohorts, but it is impossible to say with any certainty whether fluidity remained at this higher level for the third cohort.

[58] Jo Blanden, Paul Gregg & Lindsey Macmillan, 'Accounting for intergenerational income persistence' *The Economic Journal* vol.117, 2007, C45-C60. Also Jo Blanden & Stephen Machin, 'Up and down the generational income ladder in Britain' *National Institute Economic Review*, No.205, 2008, 101-116

Dividing the population into four income quartiles, Jo Blanden and her colleagues found that 42 per cent of sons born into the richest quartile of families in 1970 achieved incomes that put them in the top quartile when they grew up, while just 11 per cent ended up with incomes in the bottom quartile. For men born just twelve years earlier, however, the corresponding figures were 35 per cent and 17 per cent. In just twelve years, it seemed that kids born into more privileged backgrounds substantially increased their chances of gaining a job with a good income and significantly reduced the threat they faced of downward mobility.

The researchers summarised this shift using a 'coefficient of elasticity', a measure of the extent to which parents' incomes can predict the incomes of their children. This coefficient rose from 0.21 for the 1958 cohort to 0.29 for those born in 1970. The authors concluded from this that affluent parents must have got better at transmitting their privileged financial situation to their children. As the Chief Executive of the Sutton Trust recently explained: 'In Britain it has become increasingly the case that where you come from – who you are born to and where you are born – matters *more than ever* for where you are going.'[59]

There are a number of points to make about this claim.

The first is that it flies in the face of research on what happened to class mobility over this same period. Buscha and Sturgis measure the strength of association between class of origin and class of destination for individuals in the Household Longitudinal Survey who were born in 1958 and in 1970, and they find that it *fell* by 20 per cent. As they say, we should not necessarily expect class mobility data and earnings mobility data to reveal exactly the same pattern,

---

[59] Lee Elliot Major and Stephen Machin, *Social Mobility and its enemies* (Pelican 2018), p.19, emphasis added. Major is the Chief Executive of the Sutton Trust.

but for relative class mobility to have risen by 20 per cent while earnings mobility fell by 38 per cent looks very odd.[60]

Secondly, other researchers using other samples to analyse earnings mobility over time have failed to reproduce the Sutton Trust's result. Comparing cohorts of men in the British Household Panel Survey who were born in the crucial period between 1950 and 1972, for example, Ermisch and Nicoletti found no change in their income mobility rates. They state explicitly: 'There are no strong changes in intergenerational mobility across cohorts from 1950 to 1972.'[61] This directly contradicts the Sutton Trust findings.

Third, the Sutton Trust economists are unable to find any evidence of a continuation in the trend to reduced fluidity among people born after 1970.[62] Even if their reported findings were reliable, there are therefore no grounds for arguing (as the Social Mobility Commission and the Sutton Trust's Chief Executive both continue to do) that social mobility is *still* in decline, nor that people's origins are more important than ever in shaping their destinations. *If* this decline happened, it was a one-off drop over a single period, and it has not continued since.

Fourth, there are strong grounds for suspecting that this decline did not happen even over that one period. In

---

[60] "It is worthy of note that the mobility rates estimated by using the LS [the Household Longitudinal Survey] are not just different by degree but in the opposite direction to those of Blanden et al." Buscha and Sturgis, 'Declining social mobility?', op cit., p.174

[61] John Ermisch and Cheti Nicoletti, 'Intergenerational earnings mobility: Changes across cohorts in Britain' University of Essex, Institute for Social & Economic Research *Working Paper* No.19, 2005, p.27

[62] 'The sharp decline in intergenerational mobility that occurred between the 1958 and 1970 cohorts has not continued for more recent generations... The fall in intergenerational mobility between the 1958 and 1970 cohorts appears to have been an episode' Jo Blanden and Stephen Machin, *Recent changes in intergenerational mobility in the UK: A summary of findings* Sutton Trust, 200, p.6 https://www.suttontrust.com/wp-content/uploads/2007/12/summaryintergenerationalmobility-1.pdf

a withering critique of the Sutton Trust's methodology, Stephen Gorard notes that the research only included about one-eighth of the members of each of the two birth cohorts – the other seven-eighths were dropped because they were female (the analysis compared only fathers' and son's incomes) or because there was insufficient information about their earnings. As Gorard points out, 'The proportion of unexplained missing cases far outweighs the apparent difference between the two cohorts.'[63] He further points out that income data were collected and summarised in different ways in the 1958 and 1970 studies, and this may well have affected the income estimates which the Sutton Trust researchers rely on.

The claim that income mobility dropped precipitously between these two cohorts is also inconsistent with other evidence from these same two cohort studies. For example, there was no change in the strength of association between father's class and child's earnings (so middle class children didn't get into the top income quartile in any greater numbers in the 1970 than the 1958 cohort). Nor did the association between child's class and child's earnings change between the two studies (so those entering higher classes were no more likely to earn an income putting them in the top earnings group in the later cohort than in the earlier one).

---

[63] Stephen Gorard, 'A re-consideration of rates of social mobility in Britain' *British Journal of Sociology of Education*, vol.29, 2008, p.321. Both the 1958 and 1970 coefficients of elasticity are very weak – in both studies, more than 90 per cent of the variation in children's incomes is left unexplained by their parents' incomes (even the 1970 coefficient of 0.29 explains only 8% of the variance). In both the 1958 and 1970 surveys, about 17% of those born to the poorest quartile of families end up in the richest quartile, and vice versa. It would only need about 25 cases out of 2000 to shift between the top and bottom income quartiles for the research to comply with the ideal of a perfect meritocracy! Rather than indicating a stifling of mobility chances, Gorard says these results suggest that 'Britain has quite a staggering level of social mobility.'

Erikson and Goldthorpe speculate that the estimate of 'permanent household income' made by Blanden and her colleagues in respect of the 1958 cohort may have been faulty, in which case the association reported between parents' and childrens' incomes in this cohort would have been under-estimated.[64] Certainly, as we shall see (Truth #5, below), the incomes estimates for the UK used by the Sutton Trust here and in other publications appear very unreliable, and the Trust's own researchers have acknowledged they had problems ensuring the estimates of household incomes in the 1958 and 1970 panels were compatible.[65]

The difference between the Sutton Trust's results (a substantial fall in fluidity in just 12 years) and the results of other studies of both income and class mobility looking at the same period (all showing either no change, or a substantial increase in fluidity) is striking. At the very least, the Sutton Trust's results should clearly be treated with extreme caution. Bukodi and Goldthorpe warn that the

---

[64] Robert Erikson and John Goldthorpe 'Has social mobility in Britain decreased?' *British Journal of Sociology* vol.61, 2010, 211-30. 'The apparent cross-cohort decrease in mobility is...in some important part the result of the family income variable for the later cohort providing a better measure of permanent income than that for the earlier cohort' (p.226).

[65] Jo Blanden, Paul Gregg, Lindsey Macmillan, 'Intergenerational Persistence in Income and Social Class: The Impact of Within-Group Inequality' Centre for Market and Public Organisation *Working Paper* 11/277, University of Bristol, December 2011. The 1958 study collected separate information on mother's, father's and other income, while the 1970 survey asked only for total household income (and given that 90% of respondents were female, this required women to have accurate information about their partner's earnings). The 1958 survey also collected after-tax income while the 1970 one asked for gross income, and child benefit was explicitly included in the first but excluded in the second. The authors therefore had to adjust their estimates for all these differences and admit that 'Despite our best efforts, the resulting variables are still not completely comparable' (p.45). In addition, they admit that parental incomes in the earlier panel may have fluctuated more, making it more difficult to estimate permanent incomes. However, they believe this cannot explain more than one-tenth of the difference that they report between the two panels.

Sutton Trust's income estimates are 'as likely to mislead as to inform.'[66] Buscha and Sturgis worry about the Trust's 'thin base of evidence.'[67] David Goodhart dismisses their study as 'a slender analysis' and regrets the degree of influence it has exerted on public policy over two decades. He believes 'the lazy consensus which has decreed the end of social mobility is both wrong and damaging.'[68]

To have built an entire government social mobility strategy on the foundations of this one, rather shaky, distrusted and isolated study thus seems extremely unwise. Nevertheless, the Sutton Trust researchers have stuck by their claims, and politicians have chosen to continue to believe them.[69] Perhaps too much intellectual and political capital has been invested in this research for either the Trust or the politicians they have influenced to pull back now.

---

[66] Bukodi and Goldthorpe, *Social Mobility and Education in Britain*, p.16n

[67] Buscha and Sturgis, 'Declining social mobility?' op cit., p.155

[68] David Goodhart, 'More mobile than we think' *Prospect* 20 December 2008.

[69] Members of the Sutton Trust team continue to claim that mobility has fallen, failing to mention the controversy surrounding their claim (see for example, Lee Elliot Major and Stephen Machin, *Social Mobility and its enemies*, op cit.) Major and Machin even quote Goodhart's comment about the influence of their 'slender analysis' to boast of the continuing impact their work has on politicians (pp.26-7).

Truth #5

Britain's social mobility rate is no worse than the European average, and is better than in many other advanced industrial countries

Economists associated with the Sutton Trust not only claim that the rate of social mobility in Britain is falling. They also claim that mobility in Britain is less extensive than in other developed countries. Again, their claims have been uncritically accepted by politicians, yet again, there is a lot of research that suggests they are wrong.

Sociologists have for many years been reporting similar rates of *class mobility* across most western countries, including the UK, and any differences they have found between OECD countries have tended to be fairly small. A 1992 study by Goldthorpe and Erikson ranked England 8th out of 15 countries on a measure of 'relative mobility', with more fluidity than in Germany, France, Italy and the Netherlands, but less than in Sweden, the USA, Japan and Australia.[70] When he updated this analysis in 2004, Richard Breen confirmed that Britain still stood in the middle of the international rankings, ahead of Germany and Denmark, but behind Sweden and the USA.[71]

A 2001 review of the international evidence by the UK government's Performance and Innovation Unit concluded

---

[70] John Goldthorpe and Robert Erikson, *The Constant Flux*, Clarendon Press, 1992. Scotland and Northern Ireland performed rather worse than England.
[71] Richard Breen, *Social Mobility in Europe*, Oxford University Press, 2004

that any differences between Britain and other developed countries were 'modest'.[72] Similarly, a 2007 OECD review found that all western countries have high absolute rates of social mobility, and that Britain ranks somewhere around the middle in terms of relative rates, behind Sweden, Canada and Norway, but ahead of (West) Germany, Ireland, Italy and France.[73]

Most recently, a survey of thirty European countries, carried out between 2002 and 2010, has found that the UK is one of a cluster of countries with the highest levels of absolute mobility. Looking at relative mobility rates, the UK also comes close to being one of the most fluid. Reporting this research, Bukodi and Goldthorpe conclude: 'With relative rates of class mobility, just as with absolute rates, there is *no evidence whatever of the UK...being a low mobility society...* The UK can rather be seen as one of a fairly large number of countries that in fact share largely similar mobility regimes [with] a high level of fluidity.'[74]

In addition to class mobility, the openness of different countries can also be compared by examining their *educational mobility* rates (how well children from different social classes perform in the education system), and here too, most indicators suggest Britain is around or perhaps above average for fluidity.

The OECD ranks the UK 9th out of 30 countries on one indicator (the extent to which children's educational attainment is independent of their parents' socio-economic status), 2nd out of 17 on another (how far years of schooling

---

[72] Stephen Aldridge, *Social Mobility: A discussion paper* Cabinet Office, Performance and Innovation Unit, April 2001

[73] Anna Christina d'Addio, 'Intergenerational transmission of disadvantage' *Social, Employment and Migration Working Paper* no.52, Paris, OECD, 2007.

[74] Bukodi and Goldthorpe, *Social Mobility and Education in Britain,* p.203, emphasis added.

of parents and children differ), in the middle of the rankings on a third (the probability of a child attending university if their parents are not graduates), and 5th out of 14 on a fourth (the risk of early school leaving, comparing parents and children).[75] The UK Department of Education found in 2012 that a child's educational performance is no more predictable from its socio-economic background in England than it is in the OECD as a whole.[76] And a 2016 Sutton Trust study comparing the reading skills of 9 year-olds from the richest 10% of households with those from the poorest 10% reports that the 'social class gap' in England is around the OECD average: five countries have larger gaps than we do, four have smaller ones and two are about the same.[77]

The idea that Britain is lagging behind almost everyone else is not therefore borne out by either occupational (class) nor educational mobility statistics. It derives solely from economists' research on *income mobility*, and in particular from the work by Jo Blanden and her colleagues carried out for, and reported by, the Sutton Trust. The same team, and

---

[75] d'Addio, 'Intergenerational transmission of disadvantage', op cit., p.29. Britain's apparently favourable ranking on correlations based on years of education is, according to Blanden, due to the low variation in years of education of parents, and is therefore statistically misleading. This may be so, but it certainly doesn't place Britain at the 'immobile end' of the continuum.

[76] Analysis of children's reading scores by the UK Department for Education concludes that, while the impact of socio-economic status is somewhat greater in England than in the average OECD country (i.e. reading scores increase more as you move up the socio-economic scale in England), the strength of this association is slightly below the OECD average (i.e. knowing the parents' SES does not predict their child's reading score any better in England than in the average country). Across the OECD, socio-economic background explains 14% of the variance in children's reading scores; in England it explains 13.8%. The report concludes: 'Student attainment is no more closely related to socio-economic background than on average across the OECD.' Emily Knowles and Helen Evans, 'PISA 2009: How does the social attainment gap in England compare with countries internationally?' Department for Education *Research Report* No.206, April 2012, p.2.

[77] Sean Reardon and Jane Waldfogel, 'Learning from international comparisons' Sutton Trust *Research Brief*, 16 December 2016, p.2

the same organisation, responsible for the claim that our mobility rate has been worsening is therefore also behind the claim that our mobility rate is lower than everybody else's.

Back in 2005, Blanden and her colleagues published a hugely influential paper claiming that, when men's earnings are compared with those of their parents, Britain and the USA perform poorly compared with Canada and most other European countries. The statistical association between parents' and children's earnings in Britain was stronger than in the other nations, indicating less mobility.[78] It is this finding that has repeatedly been cited by politicians and policy makers, as well as by the Sutton Trust itself, to support the view that we have a lower social mobility rate than other countries do.[79]

The Sutton Trust researchers recognise that their results on income mobility in different countries do not tally with sociological studies of class mobility, but as with their claims about declining mobility, they have stood by their figures.[80] However, accurate income comparisons between countries are even more difficult to get right than income estimates within one country over time. With international comparisons, it is difficult to know if you are comparing like with like. Even the OECD warns that comparisons of income mobility across countries should be treated with 'a great deal of caution.'[81]

One obvious problem is that relatively few countries have carried out studies where detailed information has

---

[78] Jo Blanden, Paul Gregg, Stephen Machin, *Intergenerational mobility in Europe and North America* LSE Centre for Economic Performance, April 2005.

[79] For example: John Hills et al., *An anatomy of economic inequality in the UK* (Government Equalities Office, 2010); Major and Machin, Social Mobility and its enemies, op cit.

[80] For example: Jo Blanden, 'Cross-country rankings in inter-generational mobility' *Journal of Economic Surveys* vol.27, 2013, 38-73

[81] Anna d'Addio, 'Intergenerational transmission of disadvantage', op cit., p.29

been gathered on both parents' and children's incomes over an extended period of time. In many OECD countries, we are relying on surveys where we simply do not know what respondents' parents were earning thirty or forty years ago when they were growing up. Economists try to get around this problem by estimating what the incomes of these respondents' fathers might have been decades earlier, based on other information about them, such as what their level of education was. Needless to say, these results can be very unreliable.

A team of statisticians led by John Jerrim at London's Institute of Education has shown just how unreliable they are. Jerrim looks at countries where we do know what people's parents earned and compares the actual figures with the earnings imputed to them by using the Sutton Trust team's procedures. The correlation between people's actual ('observed') and imputed ('predicted') earnings in these countries varies between just 0.3 and 0.5, depending on which information about them is used to make the prediction. Even on the best case, this means that three-quarters of the variation in fathers' actual earnings is not accounted for by imputation. When fathers are allocated to an income quartile on the basis of their imputed earnings, only 40 per cent of them end up in the right category.[82] This is a staggeringly high level of error.

It's not just that imputation gets income estimates badly wrong; it gets them wrong in a systematically biased way. This is because imputation generally results in inflated

---

[82] John Jerrim, Alvaro Choi and Rosa Rodriguez, *Cross-national comparisons of intergenerational mobility: are the earnings measures used robust?* London, Institute of Education, October 2013. The authors calculate the Cohen's Kappa statistic to assess the reliability of the allocation of fathers to income quartiles and get results in the range of 0.13 to 0.23 – well below the 0.40 generally seen as an acceptable minimum (p.15).

estimates of the strength of association between parents' and children's earnings.[83] It is therefore telling that when the Institute of Education team looked at the strength of association between parents' and children's earnings reported across 21 countries, they found that eight of the nine countries with the lowest coefficients (i.e. the highest rates of income mobility) were those which use actual earnings data gathered from surveys.[84] Nearly all the countries with higher coefficients (indicating lower social mobility rates) used imputed earnings.

What appears to be a difference in fluidity between countries thus looks suspiciously like a difference generated by different methods for estimating parental incomes. As Jerrim and his co-authors conclude: 'Any variation found across countries could simply be due to differences in methodological approach.' They urge academics and policy makers to 'exercise a great deal of caution' when making international comparisons based on imputed data which, they warn, can 'seriously bias' findings.[85]

The UK income data used by the Sutton Trust economists are imputed. This is because they needed information about parents' 'permanent' or long-term incomes, not just a

---

[83] This is because anything that correlates with fathers' incomes (e.g. their occupation or education) is also likely to affect their sons' incomes (because, say, growing up in a middle class home increases the likelihood that you will end up getting a middle class job) – see Jo Blanden, 'Cross-country rankings', op cit., p.41.

[84] *Cross-national comparisons of intergenerational mobility*, op cit., Table 2. They are the four Nordic countries, plus Canada, Singapore, New Zealand and Germany.

[85] *Cross-national comparisons of intergenerational mobility*, op cit., p.20. One important consequence of this work is that it casts severe doubt on the claim made by the Sutton Trust and others that social mobility is more extensive in less unequal countries (the so-called 'Great Gatsby Curve' – see, for example, Major and Machin, *Social Mobility and its Enemies*, op cit., pp.34-9). Jerrim and his co-authors find that the apparent association between high inequality and low mobility disappears when countries using imputed income data are removed from the graph.

snapshot of what they happened to be earning in the week in 1958 or 1970 when an investigator called. They therefore predicted parents' long-term earnings from other things they knew about them, such as their education and their occupation, rather than relying on their reported earnings at the time of the surveys. This decision inflated the strength of association they found between parents' and children's estimated incomes, making income mobility look stickier than it really is.

Jo Blanden admits this. She and her team even deflated all the country estimates (including that for the UK) which were based on imputed earnings data by 25 per cent to try to allow for it.[86] But as Jerrim and his colleagues point out, this adjustment was little more than a guess, for we don't actually know how big the bias is.[87] Given that most of the countries using imputed data are clustered at the 'less mobile' end of the international table even after this adjustment has been made, we may well suspect that the bias is greater than 25 per cent, and that the estimates are still too high. The truth is, we simply do not know.

There are other problems, too, with the Sutton Trust's incomes data. When they came to apply their 25 per cent deflator to the British income estimates, Blanden and her team were confronted with two different surveys covering the same generation of parents which recorded very different estimates of income persistence between parents and their children. One, using the 1958 birth cohort study, gave a coefficient of 0.44 (even after being 'scaled down' from 0.58 to take account of its use of instrumental variables), a

---

[86] Scaling down by a factor 0.75 is based on US data comparing time averages with estimates using instrumental variables. Blanden accepts, 'It is a strong assumption to carry across this bias to other countries, but seems preferable to leaving the estimates uncorrected' ('Cross-country rankings...', op cit., p.45).

[87] *Cross-national comparisons of intergenerational mobility*, op cit., p.18

relatively high figure suggesting a comparatively low social mobility rate. But a second study of the same two generations of parents and children using the British Household Panel Study produced a much lower figure of just 0.29, suggesting much more fluidity. So which figure is correct?

Again, nobody knows, so Blanden averaged the two, to produce an estimate for Britain of 0.37. But this is a contrived and meaningless statistic. It was created, first, by imputing fathers' earnings rather than using reliable income sources; then by averaging the results from two widely divergent studies; and then by deflating the figure by an arbitrary one-quarter! It is on the basis of this figure that Britain is judged to have one of the worst income mobility rates in the western world.[88]

And that's not the end of the difficulties with the Sutton Trust's income statistics. Different countries collected income data on people when they were at different ages. This matters, because at 30 (when the British sample of children was asked for their incomes) people are not yet established in their careers, and their income is still likely to fluctuate significantly in the future, whereas at 40 (when the Norwegian and Finnish data were collected) people are more settled.[89] In addition, some countries combined fathers' and mothers' earnings into a single measure of parental income while others recorded only the income of the father. Godard

---

[88] Blanden compares 12 countries. Four of the five with the least mobility (the USA with a coefficient of 0.41, the UK on 0.37, Italy on 0.33 and France on 0.32) are countries where this scaling technique has been applied to their income data. The others (Norway, Australia, Germany, Sweden, Canada, Finland and Denmark) all have lower scores, but none of these estimates was imputed and adjusted.

[89] The Sutton Trust team accepts this but claims that cross-national differences still remain, even when the ages of fathers and sons in different countries are brought more into line (Jo Blanden, Paul Gregg, Stephen Machin, *Intergenerational mobility in Europe and North America*, op cit., Tables A1 and A2).

suggests father-only estimates tend to report lower inter-generational correlations, and hence more fluidity.[90]

And then there's the margins of error in the country estimates. Most have such large margins of error that it is impossible to rank them against one another with any degree of certainty. Blanden is refreshingly honest about this: 'While it is tempting to immediately form the estimates into a league table, we must pay attention to the size of the standard errors... it is impossible to statistically distinguish the estimates for Sweden and the USA. The appropriate ranking at the top end is difficult with large standard errors on the Australian, French, British and US estimates making it unclear how these countries should be ranked.'[91]

But if it is 'unclear how these countries should be ranked', how can anybody claim with any confidence that the UK has one of the worst international income mobility rates? In Blanden's sample of twelve countries, no fewer than eight (ranging from the USA with a coefficient of 0.41 to Sweden on 0.24) could be inter-changeable!

No wonder the OECD has warned that 'lack of comparable cross-country data' on income mobility means that 'comparisons can be invalid because different studies use different variable definitions, samples, estimation methods and time periods.'[92] Journalists and politicians should pay much greater heed to this warning than they have done. The international income data are virtually unusable as a basis for comparing different countries' mobility rates – yet these are the statistics on which it has confidently been asserted that Britain lags behind the rest of the developed world.

---

[90] Stephen Gorard, 'A reconsideration of rates of social mobility in Britain', op cit.

[91] Jo Blanden, 'How much can we learn from international comparisons of social mobility?' *CEE Discussion Papers* 2009, London School of Economics, p.15

[92] Osetta Causa and Asa Johansson, 'Intergenerational social mobility in OECD countries' *OECD Journal: Economic Studies*, OECD 2010, pp.2 and 9

Truth #6

The fact that middle class children are more successful than working class children in gaining middle class jobs cannot be taken as proof that they enjoy unfair advantages

There is a widespread and deeply ingrained belief held by many leading politicians and commentators that if two different social groups – be they blacks and whites, males and females, or working class and middle class kids – perform differently on average on some set of desirable outcomes – educational success, say, or income, or even things like avoiding criminality or enjoying good health – then some sort of social discrimination must be the explanation. Average differences between groups are routinely explained nowadays, not by the behaviour or characteristics of their individual members, but by the way 'society' is thought to treat them collectively.

Modern political sensibilities seem to require us to think this way. All individuals are assumed to be essentially the same, no matter which social categories they belong to, so when we discover group differences, these can only be explained by some sort of 'social injustice' operating between them. I discussed this way of thinking in my 2011 Civitas report, *The Rise of the Equalities Industry*, where I referred to it as 'the fallacy of proportionate outcomes.'[93]

---

[93] For details and data sources, see Peter Saunders, *The Rise of the Equalities Industry*, Civitas, London, 2011, chapters 8 and 9

The 'gender pay gap' is one example. The fact that men's earnings are on average higher than women's earnings is commonly cited as evidence of discrimination against female employees. But research finds that men and women on average have very different preferences in choosing careers, and very different priorities regarding work (including part-time work) and family commitments. Men tend to choose the kinds of occupations that pay more, and women often choose to take time out of the labour market to raise their children rather than keep working full-time and building their careers. Take these different preferences into account and most of the apparent 'inequality' in pay between the sexes disappears.

Infant mortality rates provide another example. Infant mortality in the Pakistani community in Britain is much higher than among whites, and the Equality and Human Rights Commission has identified this as a gross example of race-based inequality. But the Bangladeshi infant mortality rate is half that of the Pakistani one, and Bengalis in Britain are no less deprived or discriminated against than Pakistanis. The explanation is that Bengalis do not commonly marry their cousins. The high number of infant deaths among Pakistani families in Britain is almost certainly due to high rates of family in-breeding, and has nothing to do with discrimination or racism.

Policing provides a third example. Black youngsters used to be stopped and searched by police 6 or 7 times more often (relative to their population size) than whites. The Macpherson report put this down to 'racist stereotyping' by police officers, and when she was Home Secretary, Theresa May clamped down on it. But when criminologists analysed how police patrols were actually operating, they found that black kids were out on the streets much more than whites and therefore encountered police much more often. Allow for this, and the two groups were being stopped by police in equal proportions.

The 'fallacy of proportionate outcomes' has become the default explanation for policy professionals faced with average group differences, and it is therefore no surprise to find it deeply embedded within official thinking about social mobility too. Faced with evidence that middle class children are 2 or 3 times more likely than working class children to end up in middle class jobs, the automatic, knee-jerk assumption is that social factors – money, parents, contacts, prejudice, whatever – must be helping middle class children succeed while blocking those from the working class.

I call this the *SAD hypothesis* – the assumption that Social Advantages and Disadvantages are responsible for the different outcomes achieved by children from different classes.

There is, however, another possible explanation for this unequal outcome. Let us call it the *meritocracy hypothesis*. As we have seen, the meritocracy ideal (to which most politicians claim to be committed) is that talent and hard work should be the basis of rewards. Before we leap to the conclusion that some sort of discrimination is going on favouring children from some social backgrounds and discriminating against those from others, we therefore obviously need to check whether the children who fare better in the competition for educational and occupational success are on average brighter or more diligent than those who fare worse.

Is it conceivable that middle class children tend to do better in school, and to get better jobs, than working class children because, on average, they work harder, or are on average more talented? This is a possibility which many researchers and politicians find so unpalatable and offensive that they are not even prepared to consider it. For them, the meritocracy hypothesis is too shocking even to contemplate as a possibility, so they rule it out. They don't even bother asking the question. This then leaves only the SAD hypothesis as their default explanation.

The SAD hypothesis assumes there are *no* differences of ability or effort between children born into different class backgrounds. This means there should be no disparity of outcome between the classes if the system is working fairly. All children, regardless of social origins, should have exactly the same statistical chance of ending up in any given position (a disparity ratio of 1:1). Any divergence from this – any evidence that class destinations are not randomly distributed in comparison with class origins – is taken as proof that children from different class origins are being treated unfairly, and that meritocracy is therefore falling short.

This logic was central to John Goldthorpe's classic 1972 mobility survey. As we saw earlier, he found that children from professional-managerial homes were about four times more likely to end up in middle class jobs than children from working class homes. He swiftly concluded from this that 'the reality of contemporary British society most strikingly and incontrovertibly deviates from the ideal of genuine openness.'[94] Any disparity in excess of 1:1 was for him evidence that social barriers must be blocking working class children from rising and safeguarding middle class children from falling.

Goldthorpe made little attempt to identify what precisely these barriers might be, nor how they worked. He didn't need to, for he 'knew' they 'must' exist simply from the fact that the disparity ratios were so high.

---

[94] Goldthorpe, *Social Mobility and Class Structure in Modern Britain* op cit., p.114

In a book of over 300 pages, he devoted just one paragraph to considering the alternative explanation, that these disparity ratios might reflect differences of average ability or effort between the classes. He dismissed the idea as self-evidently absurd: 'Where inequalities of class chances of this magnitude are displayed,' he wrote, '*the presumption must be* that to a substantial extent they do reflect inequalities of opportunity that are rooted in the class structure, and are not simply the outcome of the differential take-up of opportunities by individuals with differing genetic, moral or other endowments.' He treated with contempt the notion that ability differences might explain his findings, labelling such explanations 'social Darwinist' and 'Smilesian'.[95]

Once governments started getting interested in social mobility around the turn of this century, the fallacy of proportionate outcomes was carried over into official thinking. Following Goldthorpe's lead, the 2001 Cabinet Office review which informed the Blair government's new social mobility strategy stipulated that a meritocratic society should be marked by 'the absence of any association between class origins and destinations.'[96] Anything greater than a 1:1 disparity ratio would constitute evidence for the continuing existence of class barriers. The idea that children from different classes might, on average, have different levels of ability or display different levels of hard work and motivation was never even considered.

Almost twenty years later, this is still the official view. In its 2019 *State of the Nation* report, the Social Mobility

---

[95] *Social Mobility and Class Structure in Modern Britain*, op cit., p.328. Social Darwinism is associated with racist theories about natural superiority and inferiority, used to justify nineteenth century imperialism, while Samuel Smiles was a Victorian liberal who believed poverty was caused mainly by irresponsible personal behaviour. For left academics like Goldthorpe, there are few insults more wounding than these.

[96] Stephen Aldridge, *Social Mobility: A Discussion Paper*, op cit., para 70.

Commission notes that working class children are twice as likely as middle class children to end up in working class jobs. It deduces from this the existence of what it calls an 'entrenched sticky floor' which is preventing working class kids from rising. Similarly, the fact that children from professional-managerial homes are almost twice as likely as working class children to end up in middle class jobs is explained by a 'sticky ceiling' which helps them hold on to their privileges and 'squeeze out' those from less advantaged backgrounds.[97] The possibility that some or all of this apparent 'stickiness' might be accounted for by class-based variations in ability or effort is never seriously considered. Just like Goldthorpe almost fifty years earlier, the very idea is for the Commission self-evidently ridiculous.

In a democratic age increasingly obsessed with not giving offence to any group, the suggestion that social classes may already have been sorted, at least to some extent, on the basis of ability differences is politically unwelcome, and perhaps even unmentionable. Politicians find it much easier to tell people they have been unfairly shut out of access to good jobs than to explain to them that they just weren't bright enough (or sufficiently hard-working) to qualify for one. This undoubtedly helps explain why the meritocratic explanation has so rarely been seriously examined.

But it is not without irony that politicians who say they are committed to achieving a 'meritocracy' are too scared to ask how far ability and personal effort may already be shaping social mobility outcomes.

---

[97] Social Mobility Commission, *State of the Nation 2018-19* op cit., pp.3-4

Truth #7

Cognitive ability (IQ) is at least 50 per cent genetic and social class advantages and disadvantages hardly affect it

If we want to test the meritocracy hypothesis, rather than just dismiss it out of hand, then we obviously need to measure the ability levels of individuals who get recruited into different social classes. Different kinds of abilities are required for different kinds of jobs, but for jobs in management and the professions requiring high levels of numeracy, literacy, logical judgement and reasoning skills, intellectual ability is likely to be crucial. Measuring intellectual ability means using IQ tests or similar cognitive assessments.

Intellectual or cognitive ability has various dimensions, but psychologists commonly measure it by a single statistic, the IQ score. Because different kinds of mental abilities correlate with each other, it is possible to identify a common factor, 'general intelligence' (g), and it is this that IQ tests seek to measure. Just as we might speak of a general quality of 'athleticism' shared in common by those who are good at sprinting, marathon running and long jumping, so too we can identify a common factor of intelligence shared by people with good spatial ability, verbal ability, mathematical ability, logical reasoning ability, and so on.[98]

---

[98] 'There are distinctions between tests of verbal and spatial ability, abstract reasoning and speed of information processing, but...these tests all correlate positively with one another. It is, therefore, at best misleading to say that these tests measure wholly independent abilities. More plausibly, they measure a set of overlapping processes whose importance varies from one kind of test to another.' N. Mackintosh, 'Insight into intelligence' *Nature* (vol.377, 19 Oct 1995), p.582

IQ scores, computed from the results of various kinds of cognitive tests, are expressed on a normalised scale with a mean of 100 and a standard deviation of 15. In other words, the average IQ score in the population is set at 100, with roughly two-thirds of people scoring in the range 85-115, and 95 per cent scoring between 70 and 130.

There is a long history of controversy surrounding the interpretation of IQ scores.[99] Critics have frequently rejected the idea of 'general intelligence,' dismissed the possibility that cognitive ability might have any innate or biological foundation, and insisted that IQ tests are culture-bound and class-biased.[100] However, most of these judgements have been shown over time to be ill-informed and ill-founded.[101]

IQ scores clearly measure something real. They are remarkably stable over long periods of time (one Scottish study re-tested men and women at age 77 and found a correlation of 0.73 with their test scores at age 11).[102] They correlate strongly with results of other tests of mental skills, such as reading and maths tests (i.e. they achieve 'external validity'), as well as with each other (they achieve 'internal

---

[99] For a review, see Gary Marks, *Education, social background and cognitive ability*, Routledge 2015, chapter 4.

[100] For a review from both sides of the debate, see *Intelligence: The Battle for the Mind: H.J. Eysenck Versus Leon Kamin* (Pan Macmillan, 1981).

[101] James Heckman says critics of IQ research, like Kamin and Gould, 'rely heavily on innuendo', ignore evidence on the predictive power of IQ scores, and peddle the idea that IQ tests are culture-biased with little or no justification (James Heckman, 'Lessons from the Bell Curve' *The Journal of Political Economy*, vol.103, 1995, p.1096). See also: Linda Gottfredson, 'Mainstream Science on Intelligence: An Editorial with 52 signatories, history and bibliography', *Intelligence, 1997*, vol. 24, pp. 13-23; and Robert Plomin and Ian Deary,'Genetics and intelligence differences: five special findings', *Molecular Psychiatry*, vol.20, 2014, pp. 98–108.

[102] The authors claim even this under-estimates the true strength of association, due to the effects of measurement error. See Ian Deary and others, 'The stability of individual differences in mental ability from childhood to old age' *Intelligence* vol.28, 2000, 49-55.

validity').[103] They are good predictors of other measures of mental alacrity such as reaction times (e.g. how long it takes you to push a button after a light flashes), inspection times (e.g. how long you need to recognise which of two lines is longer), working memory capacity (how much information you can retain while working on something else), and forward and backward digit span test results (the ability to repeat a sequence of numbers forwards relative to the ability to repeat the same sequence backwards).[104] IQ scores also correlate with directly measured brain activity such as the evoked potentials of brainwaves (the speed of brain waves evoked by sudden stimuli of light or sound), positron emission topography (the amount of glucose used by the brain when solving problems), and the highly heritable condition of myopia.[105] In short, they are measuring real and enduring differences between people's intellectual capacities.

We know that children's IQ scores correlate fairly strongly with those of their parents. Research from samples around

---

[103] See for example: Michael O'Connell, 'The power of cognitive ability in explaining educational test performance, relative to other ostensible contenders' *Intelligence*, vol.66, 2018. pp. 122-127

[104] The fact that IQ correlates with forward and backward digit span test results enables us to rule out differential motivation as a possible cause of variations in IQ scores, for subjects will be no less motivated calculating backward than forward sequences, but it is the latter that correlates with IQ: See Richard Herrnstein and Charles Murray, *The Bell Curve* (New York, Free Press, 1994).

[105] Phenomena like reaction times, brainwave potentials, and positron emissions relate directly to brain processing speed, accuracy and efficiency – factors which are central to intellectual capacity. See Herrnstein and Murray for a discussion of experiments based on forward and backward digit span tests and reaction time tests (*The Bell Curve*, op cit., pp.282-6), and Hans Eysenck, 'Clever measures' (*Times Higher Education Supplement*, 27 January 1995) for a discussion of positron emission topography. Much of this research is also reviewed by Daniel Casse, 'IQ since the Bell Curve' *Journal of Psychometric Science* (August 1998, 27-37), who concludes that, 'General intelligence as a psychological trait is on a more solid foundation than is enjoyed by any other aspect of personality or behaviour.'

the world has found that on average, children's IQ scores correlate with those of their mothers or fathers at or around 0.5 (a correlation of 0.5 means that a parent's IQ predicts on average 25 per cent of their child's IQ).[106] Taking both parents together, the average correlation with children's IQ scores is around 0.7.[107]

In the 1958 UK birth cohort study, children's cognitive ability was measured by tests at age 7 and 11. Years later, when they became parents themselves, their children were also tested. The ability scores of the parents when they were children were found to correlate strongly and significantly with the scores achieved by their children when they reached 7; a result which the researchers describe as 'remarkable.'[108]

Of course, just because bright parents often produce bright children doesn't necessarily mean it's because of the genes they pass on to them ('nature') – it could be because of the way they raise them ('nurture'). It is theoretically possible that higher IQ parents might offer more intellectual

---

[106] The square of a correlation coefficient is the proportion of variance explained in the dependent variable.

[107] Anna Christina d'Addio reports an average correlation of 0.5 between parents and children based on 212 different studies ('Intergenerational transmission of disadvantage' op cit., p.24). Plomin finds an average correlation between parental cognitive ability (mostly mothers) and their biological child, based on 8000 pairs, of 0.42 (Robert Plomin, John DeFries, Valerie Knopik, and Jenae Neiderhiser, *Behavioural Genetics*, sixth edn, Worth Publishers, 2013, p. 195). The father-child ability correlation is between 0.4 and 0.5 (Sandra Black, Paul Devereux and Kjell Salvanes, 'Like Father, Like Son? A Note on the Intergenerational Transmission of IQ Scores', *NBER Working Paper No. 14274*, 2009; Erik Grönqvist, Bjorn Öckert, and Jonas Vlachos, 'The intergenerational transmission of cognitive and non-cognitive abilities', *Human Resources* vol.52, 2016). If both parents are considered together, the average correlation between average parent ability and the average ability of their children (based on 3 studies) is around 0.72 (Thomas Bouchard and Matthew McGue, 'Familial studies of intelligence: A review', Science, vol. 212, 1981, pp. 1055-1059).

[108] Fernando Galindo-Rueda and Anna Vignoles, *Class Ridden or Meritocratic? An economic analysis of recent changes in Britain* London School of Economics Centre for the Economics of Education, May 2003,p.32.

stimulation to their children, for example, and this could then result in their children recording higher IQ scores.

However, we have known for a long time that intelligence is at least 50 per cent 'heritable' – i.e. at least 50 per cent of the difference between people's IQ scores is explained by their genetic inheritance, their DNA. We know this because of repeated experiments comparing the IQ scores of individuals who are genetically related to each other and who grow up in different environments with those of unrelated individuals growing up in shared environments.[109]

The strongest experiments compare the performance on ability tests of identical (monozygotic) twins as compared with non-identical (dizygotic) twins. MZ twins share all their genes in common while DZ twins share 50% of their genes. Forty years ago, Hans Eysenck reviewed the evidence from various studies around the world and reported average correlations in intelligence test scores of 0.87 for MZ twins raised in the same environment, 0.77 for MZ twins reared in separate environments, and 0.53 for DZ twins raised in the same environment. These figures compared with an average correlation of 0.23 for biologically unrelated individuals who were raised in a common environment (e.g. adopted or foster children), and a zero correlation for unrelated children raised in different environments.[110]

These figures point to the existence of a substantial genetic component to intelligence, for variations attributable to separate environments are much lower than those

---

[109] See Hans Eysenck, *The Inequality of Man* (op cit.); D. Fulker and H. Eysenck, *The Structure and Measurement of Intelligence* (New York, Springer-Verlag, 1979); H. Eysenck versus L. Kamin, *Intelligence: The battle for the mind* (op cit.); R. Plomin, *Blueprint*, op cit., chapter 4.

[110] In Eysenck versus Kamin, *op cit.* Similar figures are reported in Richard Herrnstein, *IQ in the Meritocracy* (Boston, Little, Brown & Co, 1973) who also lists correlation coefficients for different types of blood relatives.

attributable to different genetic inheritance. Critics have repeatedly attempted to dispute this by suggesting that the experimental conditions on which these results depend were often flawed. Kamin, for example, suggests (probably rightly) that twins who are raised separately are often nevertheless brought up in similar environments, and this will tend to underestimate the contribution of environmental factors because the degree of environmental variation is relatively small.

In the end, however, these criticisms appear trifling in face of the fact that IQ test scores for MZ twins reared apart correlate much more strongly than those of DZ twins reared together.[111] No matter how great or small the variations in environmental conditions, if environment were more important than heredity the relative strength of these correlations would be reversed.

In psychology (as in any social science), identifying a single cause that explains 50 per cent of the variance in some characteristic is almost unprecedented, so the fact that IQ has been shown to be at least 50 per cent heritable is a remarkably strong finding.[112] So which genes are responsible?

For some years after scientists succeeded in mapping the human genome, researchers looked in vain to locate what they thought would be a small number of genes linked to IQ. For a long time they couldn't find them, and this encouraged sceptics (like sociologist, John Goldthorpe) to

---

[111] M. Daniels, B. Devlin and K. Roeder, 'Of Genes and IQ', in Devlin et al., eds., *Intelligence, Genes, and Success: Scientists respond to the Bell Curve* (New York: Springer-Verlag, 1997, p.56); Plomin et al., *Behavioral Genetics* (op cit.), p.195

[112] 'Few effect sizes in psychology are greater than 5 per cent... This is why it is incredible to find that 50 per cent of the differences between people in psychological traits are caused by genetic differences between them. The heritability effect size of 50 per cent is off the scale of effect sizes in psychology' Robert Plomin, *Blueprint*, op cit., p.30

suggest that the genetic basis of intelligence may have been exaggerated.[113] However, we now know that intelligence (like other personality variations) depends on thousands of tiny variations in people's DNA (what biologists call 'polygenicity'). We also know that each of these tiny DNA variations in turn affects a lot more than just our intelligence ('pleitotropy').[114]

As of 2018, genome-wide association (GWA) studies had succeeded in identifying around 200 DNA variations (single nucleotide polymorphisms, or SNPs) associated with IQ scores. The average effect size of each of these associations is just 0.01 per cent of the total variance in IQ scores across the population. This means we still need to identify thousands more SNP associations before we get to the 50 per cent of variance which we know from twins and other research is the heredity level of IQ. This will require some huge samples.[115]

The problem is that researchers do not have samples of hundreds of thousands of people where every individual has not only given their DNA, but has also undertaken an IQ test. For this reason, they tend to focus on proxies of intelligence, such as educational attainment (which correlates at around 0.5 with IQ), and look for SNPs associated with that.

---

[113] Burkodi, Erikson and Goldthorpe, 'The effects of social origins', pp.6-7

[114] Robert Plomin, *Blueprint*, op cit., p.70. We all share about 99% of our DNA in common, but about 1 in every thousand nucleotides in a strand of DNA differs between people (its chemical base varies between different individuals in the population). These distinctive nucleotides are called single nucleotide polymorphisms, or SNPs, and most people's DNA contains about 4 or 5 million of them. Most of these SNPs have lots of tiny effects, so to find how variations in DNA may be causing particular variations in the population (e.g. variations in IQ scores), we need to compare the DNA of hundreds of thousands of individuals. We can then create 'polygenic scores' for each individual based on the number and weighting of relevant SNPs present in their DNA, and these scores can then be correlated with whatever characteristic it is that we are investigating.

[115] *Blueprint*, p.131

Analysing data from some huge samples, behavioural geneticists have constructed people's 'polygenic scores' (often aggregating hundreds of thousands or even millions of tiny SNPs) which correlate with indicators of educational attainment such as years of education. By 2018, they had succeeded in explaining 11–13% of the variance in educational attainment (and 7–10% of the variance in cognitive performance) by these polygenic scores.[116] It is likely that these figures will increase in the future with larger samples and improved methods.

So we now know – and can prove – that IQ scores are strongly based in genetics.[117]

Grasping at straws, sociologists who are disinclined to accept the importance of genetics have often emphasised the remaining 50 per cent of variance in IQ scores which is unexplained by our genes. Doesn't this suggest that IQ is as much the product of people's social class background (the environmental conditions of their upbringing) as of their genetic inheritance? Robert Plomin gives two reasons why this is not the case.

---

[116] J. Lee, et al., 'Gene discovery and polygenic prediction from a genome-wide association study of educational attainment in 1.1 million individuals', *Nature Genetics*, vol.50, 2018, pp. 1112-1121

[117] Inevitably, some social scientists continue to contest this. Ken Richardson and Michael Jones ('Why genome-wide associations with cognitive ability measures are probably spurious', *New Ideas in Psychology*, vol.55, 2019, 35-41) suggest that the association between IQ/educational performance and polygenic scores could be explained if different ancestral groups (with distinctive DNA profiles) have clustered in the same social class positions over multiple generations (e.g. due to discrimination). IQ and education scores might then reflect historically advantaged or disadvantaged social positions rather than DNA. Similarly, these same authors suggest that the clear association that has been found between polygenic scores and the educational performance of siblings (brothers and sisters with higher scores do better – see Truth #11) could be due to parents and teachers responding more positively to children with genetic characteristics which happen to correlate with SNPs associated with educational success. Reading stuff like this, one hears the distinctive sound of barrel bottoms being scraped and straws being clutched.

He points out, first, that 'environmental' influences on IQ (and, indeed, on other personality traits) are almost entirely random and seem to have nothing to do with the kind of family background people come from. The sorts of things sociologists like to think might influence cognitive ability – an affluent home, supportive parenting, expensive schooling – make hardly any difference to people's cognitive ability scores. We know this because IQ differences between adult siblings vary just as much when they have been raised together as when they have been raised apart. While it is true that IQ is not solely genetic, almost everything about it that is not genetic is down to chance events that we can't explain or predict. Parenting and home environment have almost nothing to do with it.[118]

Second, Plomin notes that what may appear to be 'environmental' effects on IQ (or on other aspects of personality) often turn out themselves to be partly driven by our genes. This is because we seek out environmental stimuli which are consistent with our genetic abilities and predispositions. We are happiest and most fulfilled when engaging in the activities for which our natural talents and

---

[118] Plomin reports that the average difference in IQ scores between siblings is 13 points, which is not much less than the average 17 points difference you will find between any two individuals selected at random from the population. The *only* reason siblings' scores are a bit more similar is because they share some of their genes in common (because they have the same parents). Take away these shared genes and their scores would differ as much as those of any two strangers. This means that, 'Growing up in the same family with someone does not make you resemble them beyond your genetic similarity… we would be just as similar to our parents and our siblings even if we had been adopted at birth and reared in different families… far from the family being a monolithic determinant of who we are, environmental influences shared by family members *do not make a difference*' (*Blueprint*, op cit., p.73). This does not mean that particular events in the lives of particular individuals do not make a difference (abuse, neglect and so on obviously can and do have long-lasting, traumatic effects). But at the level of the population as a whole, family influences are too weak to leave a measurable effect.

propensities best suit us, and over time, the more we engage in these activities, the more we develop these capacities.

Plomin calls this process of genetically-driven selection of environmental influences 'the nature of nurture,' and he estimates that about half of the apparent 'environmental' effect on personality traits like ability can be explained in this way. This is why heritability of intelligence increases as people get older (from about 40 per cent in childhood to over 60 per cent in adulthood, giving an overall average of 50 per cent).[119] We get better at the things we were born to be good at because we practice them more.[120] Or as Plomin puts it, we 'grow into' our genes.

---

[119] Research on identical twins finds stronger associations between them when they reach adulthood than when they are children. Plomin, *Blueprint*, op cit., p.52-3

[120] Again, sociologists disinclined to endorse theories based in genetics have jumped on this interaction effect between genes and environment to claim that, if genes differ in their expression across different environments, the impact on IQ of non-genetic effects may be much greater than 50% (see, for example, Bukodi, Erikson and Goldthorpe, 'The effects of social origins...', op cit., p.7, or Bukodi and Goldthorpe, *Social mobility and education in Britain*, p.110). But the effect actually operates in the other direction, increasing the impact of genes (which is why genetic effects strengthen rather than weaken as we get older). Plomin shows, for example, that about half of the correlation between environmental measures and psychological traits can be accounted for by genetics (*Blueprint*, p.51). It is not that nature and nurture are indistinguishable (as suggested by Bukodi et al.'s claim that the distinction is 'obsolete' or 'scientifically outmoded', or Bukodi and Goldthorpe's claim that it is 'no longer tenable'), but rather that genes explain a large chunk of what used to be thought of as 'environmental' effects. Bukodi and Goldthorpe seem to misunderstand the 'nature of nurture' effect. It doesn't undermine heritability estimates; it strengthens them.

TRUTH #8

Bright working class children do not suddenly get overtaken in tests by dull middle class children (although a lot of politicians, journalists and academics claim that they do)

Before proceeding further, it is important to consider one piece of research that has been widely quoted and cited by politicians and journalists as well as academics because it seems to show, consistently with the SAD hypothesis, that class background has a startling effect on the early development of cognitive ability.

Leon Feinstein's 2003 analysis of children from the 1970 birth cohort claimed that many working class children born with high ability experienced a dramatic slow-down in their cognitive development between the ages of 2 and 4 as social disadvantages started to hold them back. Meanwhile, less bright children born to more affluent parents caught up, and then overtook them. The only explanation seemed to be that early in childhood, social background smothers natural ability, which would mean that IQ measured later in childhood and in adulthood would strongly reflect early class-based social advantages and disadvantages.[121]

---

[121] Social inequalities appear to dominate the apparent early positive signs of academic ability for most of those low SES children who do well early on' Leon Feinstein, 'Very early evidence' *Centre for Economic Performance Paper* No.146, June 2003, London School of Economics, p.30

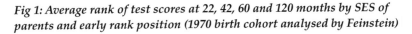

Fig 1: Average rank of test scores at 22, 42, 60 and 120 months by SES of parents and early rank position (1970 birth cohort analysed by Feinstein)

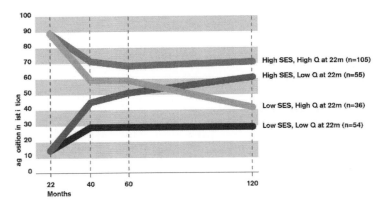

Feinstein summarised his evidence in a famous and much-celebrated graph (Figure 1).[122] It plots test scores for a small sample of children when they were 22, 40, 60 and 120 months old.[123] It suggests that initially bright working class children (the 'Low SES, High Q' trend line) tend to fall back in the early years of life, while initially dull middle class children ('High SES, Low Q') make up ground. Before long, they change places in the cognitive pecking order, and this divergence in their ability levels is then likely to shape the rest of their lives.

---

[122] *The Guardian* eulogised him: 'Inside government, a man called Leon Feinstein is feted. A civil servant at the Treasury, he is a well-liked, diligent academic – brown suits and unwittingly trendy stubble with a "shed-load of integrity". Universities minister David Willetts is a fan, and all introduce him almost as if introducing his namesake minus the F. Feinstein is the man who created the Graph: it shows that poor bright kids fall behind rich but not so bright kids by the age of 10. It was pride of place in Clegg's social mobility strategy' (Allegra Stratton, 'David Davis takes up challenge to prepare next round of Tory policies' *The Guardian*, 14 April 2011).

[123] Different kinds of exercises were set at different ages (at 22 months, the children were asked to put on their shoes, stack cubes and point to their eyes; at 42 months, they were tested on counting and speaking skills and were asked to draw assorted shapes; copying and vocabulary tests were given at age 5; and reading and maths were tested at 10).

Even the earliest scores at 22 months varied by the occupational status of the children's parents. Those whose parents were in professional-managerial occupations achieved an average ranking at the 55th per centile while those with parents in semi- or unskilled manual occupations ranked on average at the 42nd. But from then on, the former group seemed to get stronger over time while the latter's scores deteriorated. So bad did it become that initially high scoring working class children (the 'Low SES, High Q' group in Figure 1) were eventually overtaken by initially low scoring middle class children ('High SES, Low Q') at some point between 5 and 10 years of age.

Appalled by this, Michael Gove, then Education Secretary, told a Commons Select Committee in 2010 that, 'Rich thick kids do better than poor clever children when they arrive at school, and the situation as they go through gets worse.'[124] His comment got a lot of publicity. But it wasn't true.

The problem with Feinstein's analysis was he forgot to take account of what statisticians call 'regression to the mean.' Any cognitive test result (not least a test administered at just 22 months old) will offer only an approximate estimate of a child's true ability (i.e. every score will include some element of 'measurement error'). In a one-off test, some children will score much higher or lower than they usually would. This creates two problems in his graph.

First, when children are separated into groups of high and low scorers on the basis of a single test, as they were in Feinstein's study, some of those assigned to the high ability group will actually have over-achieved, and some of those assigned to the low ability group will have under-achieved.

---

[124] Graeme Paton, '"Rich thick kids do better at school" says Gove' *Daily Telegraph* 28 July 2010.

In later tests, the over-achievers will tend to score lower and the under-achievers will tend to score higher (reflecting their true ability levels).

Secondly, the problem of over-estimated ability scores will be greatest among the lower class 'high ability' group, and the problem of under-estimated ability scores will be greatest among the higher-class, 'low ability' group. This is because average IQ scores are lower among lower-class children. There are therefore likely to be more low ability, lower-class children registering unusually high scores in a one-off test, and more high ability, higher-class children registering unusually low scores.

In later tests, children who scored much higher or lower than expected given their true ability are unlikely to repeat their extreme scores (although a few might). Most of the abnormally high scorers from the first test will therefore appear to 'lose ability' in a second and later tests, while many abnormally low scorers first time around will appear to 'gain' it. It's not that their ability has changed; it's simply that fluke scores rarely get repeated.

According to John Jerrim and Anna Vignoles, this explains the Feinstein graph.[125] They demonstrate that this is the case using a series of test results taken by a sample of children in the Millennium survey (a cohort of children born in 2000).

At the age of 3, children in the Millennium survey were given two different ability tests: The British Ability Scale (based on a literacy test) and the Bracken School Readiness Test. When the results from the first of these tests are plotted on a graph together with test results taken at later ages,

---

[125] John Jerrim and Anna Vignoles, 'The use and misuse of statistics in understanding social mobility' Department of Quantitative Social Science *Working Paper*, no.11-01, April 2011, Institute of Education, London

we get the same pattern as in Feinstein's research on the 1970 cohort (Fig 2a). Indeed, on this occasion, low scoring children from affluent homes (designated by the circle symbol) appear to catch up with high scoring children from poor homes (the diamond symbol) by the age of 7.

Fig.2: Average rank of test scores of children in the Millennium Cohort Study (a) based on a single test score at 22 months and (b) correcting for regression to the mean by substituting a second set of test results to classify high and low ability groups (Jerrim and Vignoles)

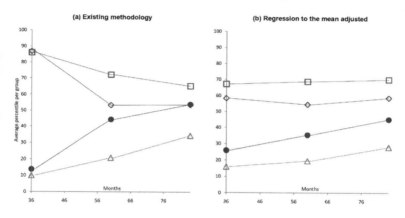

But then Jerrim and Vignoles re-ran the analysis, this time allocating children to high or low ability groups using one set of ability scores (the school readiness test), then using the other set (the British Ability Scale) to plot their initial scores at age 3, thereby avoiding the problem of regression to the mean. As can be seen in Fig.2b, the familiar pattern disappeared. There was now no sign of the ability scores of bright children from poor homes (the diamond line) declining over time. Their initial scores were on average much lower than before (the initial average ranking near the 90th per centile has fallen to 60th), and their scores stayed more-or-less at that level from age 3 to 5 to 7.

This demonstrates that the famous cross-over of bright working class and dull middle class children in Feinstein's study was the result of regression to the mean caused by measurement error in the earliest test. As Jerrim and Vignoles conclude: 'There is currently an overwhelming view amongst academics and policymakers that highly able children from poor homes get overtaken by their affluent (but less able) peers before the end of primary school. Although this empirical finding is treated as a stylised fact, the methodology used to reach this conclusion is seriously flawed. After attempting to correct for the aforementioned problem, we find little evidence that this is actually the case in current data.'[126]

The fact that Feinstein's claims have been shown to be false does not mean that social class advantages and disadvantages count for nothing – there is evidence in Feinstein's work that children from high SES backgrounds do tend to strengthen their performance on tests over time, whether they scored high or low initially, and this can also be seen in the Jerrim and Vignoles graph. But the shift is not dramatic, it may not endure long-term, and as has been shown in other research, it has nothing to do with their cognitive ability scores changing.[127]

---

[126] 'The use and misuse of statistics in understanding social mobility' op cit., p.22

[127] Analysing the progress of half a million children from Key Stage 1 (age 5) through to A-levels and university entry, Claire Crawford and two co-authors control for the problem of regression to the mean but still find that the academic success of children from deprived backgrounds who score high on Stage 1 tests tends to tail off later in their school careers. However, this happens mainly after they start secondary school (not when they are very young, as Feinstein thought), it shows up in exam results rather than IQ test scores, and they are never overtaken by those Michael Gove called 'the rich thick kids' (the least deprived children who got average scores at age 5 eventually catch them up by the time they all take GCSEs at 16, but the least deprived low-scoring kids at 5 never get anywhere near them). These results suggest that our state secondary schools could do better in nurturing the talent and maintaining the motivation of their most able lower class students – but the trashing of working

Unfortunately, it is one thing to demonstrate that a cherished result like the Feinstein graph is flawed, but quite another to get left-wing journalists, politicians and academics to take this on board. *The Guardian* was furious when Feinstein's results were exposed as false, reporting the news under the headline: *Poor children's life chances face a new assault from the right.*[128] And eight years after the study was shown to be flawed, the *New Statesman* was still telling its readers: 'As the work of Leon Feinstein, director of evidence at the Children's Commissioner office, has shown, bright but poor children are overtaken by their less gifted but more fortunate peers at the age of six.'[129] It's not true, but they're still saying it.

So are the academics and think tank policy wonks, and they really should know better. In 2018 (seven years after Feinstein's result had been shown to be false), the Chief Executive of the Sutton Trust, Lee Elliot Major, co-authored a book which reproduced the famous graph. He said it proved that, 'The academic race is over for many children when they have barely started primary school.'[130] He acknowledged that, 'Researchers have questioned the reliability... suggesting these patterns may reflect the "regression to the mean" effect.' But then he ignored his own warning and reproduced the graph as if it were valid. He concluded: 'Feinstein's graph remains a powerful portrayal

---

class talent in the early years of life (suggested by Feinstein's startling results) simply does not occur. Claire Crawford, Lindsey MacMillan, Anna Vignoles, *Progress made by high-attaining children from disadvantaged backgrounds*, Social Mobility Commission Research Report, 2014, Figure 9

[128] Fiona Millar 'Poor children's life chances face a new assault from the right' *The Guardian* 14 June 2011.

[129] *New Statesman* editorial, 'The 7 Per Cent Problem' 30 January 2019

[130] Major and Machin, *Social mobility and its enemies*, op cit., p.92

of how in early life talent can apparently decline for children from poorer backgrounds.'[131]

But how can a graph 'remain a powerful portrayal' of something when it is erroneous and misleading? The Sutton Trust is a trusted player in this field. It has long had the ear of government. Lee Elliot Major is its Chief Executive. Yet he reproduced material he knew to be false to support an argument that isn't true.

Feinstein's flawed graph is similarly still being used by left-wing academics as if it had never been falsified. In his 2017 book on social mobility in Britain, for example, sociologist Geoff Payne reports Feinstein's 'findings' as if they were valid. He offers no warning of the methodological flaws even though he was certainly aware of them.[132]

The reason left-wing researchers are loath to abandon Feinstein's graph is because it gives them the excuse they need to discredit and ignore IQ scores. Take, for example, Freedman and Laurison's research on social mobility into top professional positions. They admit they have no information on the IQ scores of the successful people analysed in their study, but they insist this doesn't matter because, they say, Feinstein's work has proved that IQ is nothing but a 'proxy' for social privilege. Knowing these people's IQ scores would, they say, tell them nothing over and above what they already know from looking at their class origins.[133]

---

[131] Major and Machin, *Social mobility and its enemies*, op cit., p.94

[132] Geoff Payne, *The new social mobility* op cit., p.145. Payne references my 2012 paper, 'Social mobility delusions', in which I discuss the problem in Feinstein's results at some length, so he must have been aware of the issue. He just doesn't mention it.

[133] 'Feinstein showed that while there are important differences in performance on educational tests between children at age 2, these initial differences then shift strongly according to the children's class background as they get older…

This reasoning is fatuous. If you want to explain these people's success, of course it would be useful to have some measure of how talented they are. But in academia, as in the policy world, researchers are reluctant to drop a 'finding,' such as Feinstein's, which fits their ideological leanings so perfectly, even when they know it is totally false.

This suggests that even if genetic differences exist between children, they are then heavily magnified by highly classed patterns of socialisation…Measures of intelligence like IQ are in many ways proxies for social endowments passed on through socialisation rather than through genetics and therefore cannot be parsed from class origin" Sam Friedman and Daniel Laurison, *The class ceiling: Why it pays to be privileged* (Kindle edition, 2019), locations 4787-94

Truth #9

The different rates of occupational success achieved by children from different class backgrounds are consistent with what would happen if recruitment were based solely on ability

We have known for a long time that average IQ levels vary by social class. Analysis of the 1958 and 1970 UK birth cohort studies reveals correlations of around 0.35 between men's social class positions and their IQ scores, with correlations slightly higher for women.[134]

Results like these should not surprise us. In each generation, average IQ scores vary across different social classes because people get jobs (and hence end up in social class positions) partly on the basis of their cognitive ability. Employers do not recruit people randomly; they generally try to attract the best people they can get, which usually means appointing the brightest people with the strongest qualifications to the highest positions.[135] The more open and meritocratic the country is, the stronger will be the link between class and intelligence, because more people will be selected this way, and fewer will be chosen simply because of their background, contacts or parentage.

---

[134] Gary Marks, *Education, social background and cognitive ability*, op cit., p.97

[135] Michelle Jackson ('Non-meritocratic job requirements and the reproduction of class inequality' *Work, Employment & Society* vol.15, 2001, 619-30) suggests on the basis of a content analysis of job advertisements that: 'It is clear that merit characteristics are important for employers' (p.624), and this is true at all occupational levels.

The strong link between class and IQ is further reinforced because successful, bright men and women often end up mating with each other (many of us meet our future partners at university or through work). When intelligent women mate with intelligent men, the result tends often to be intelligent children (although not necessarily as bright as their parents). Conversely, men and women of lower intelligence also often end up together, and they tend to produce children with relatively lower average IQs (although not necessarily as low as their parents').[136]

Given that IQ is at least 50 per cent genetic, and is transmitted to a significant extent from parents to children, we should therefore *expect* that children born into working class homes (where average levels of intelligence are lower) will tend to have lower IQ scores than children born into the middle class (where average levels of intelligence are higher). And this is exactly what we do find. Researchers in Britain in the 1950s (when IQ tests were routinely administered to children, and sociologists were generally happy to use the results in their research) recorded average IQ scores of 109 for middle class children as compared with 98 for working class children.[137]

It follows from this that, in meritocratic conditions, middle class children will do better on average than working class children in the competition for middle class jobs. Not

---

[136] S. Preston and C. Campbell, 'Differential fertility and the distribution of traits: The case of IQ' (*American Journal of Sociology*, vol.98, 1993, pp.997-1019), table 2. Because there is not a perfect correlation between parents' and children's IQs, more children of high IQ parents will score a bit lower than their parents than will score higher (because very few individuals score extremely high in any generation),and more children of low IQ parents will likewise score slightly higher than their parents (because very few score extremely low). In each generation, IQ scores therefore 'regress towards the mean.'

[137] A. Halsey, A. Heath, J. Ridge, *Origins and Destinations: Family, Class and Education in Modern Britain* (Oxford, Clarendon Press, 1980).

because they have unfair advantages, but because they are, on average, brighter. Seen in this light, the question for social mobility research is not why there is a disparity ratio between the classes in excess of 1:1; it is how big a disparity should there be if the society were operating purely on meritocratic principles, selecting people only on the basis of their ability?

When Anthony Heath re-analysed Goldthorpe's data from his 1972 study, adding imputed IQ scores of 109 for the sons of middle class fathers, and 98 for sons born into the working class, he found that a significant chunk of the 4:1 disparity ratio in their eventual social class destinations fell away. There were moderately strong associations between the (imputed) IQ of sons and their level of educational success ($r=0.38$), and between their imputed IQ and their occupational success ($r=0.27$), and these considerably weakened the link reported by Goldthorpe between class origins and class destinations. Indeed, Heath concluded: 'Those circumstances of birth which we can measure do not exert a very powerful constraint on...later achievements.'[138]

In reality of course, not all the sons in Goldthorpe's study did have IQ scores of 109 (if they came from the middle class) or 98 (if they came from the working class). A different approach was taken by Geoff Payne who noted that around 40 per cent of children born to professional-managerial class parents are downwardly mobile despite the advantages they enjoy. He deduced from this that no more than 60 per cent of middle class children can be born with the ability required to gain middle class jobs. Assuming (like Goldthorpe) that ability is equally distributed across the classes, he argued that this meant that up to 60 per cent of working class children must be born with the talent needed to get into the

---

[138] Anthony Heath, *Social Mobility*, Fontana, 1981, p.165.

middle class, even though fewer than 30 per cent actually make it. This meant that 1 in 7 people (15 per cent of the population) was being consigned to the 'wrong' class in any one generation.[139] Most people end up where their ability suggests they should be, but a significant minority does not.

The problem with Payne's estimate, of course, is that cognitive ability is not equally distributed between the classes. We have seen that it gets transmitted (at least to some extent) from parents to children (it is 50 per cent heritable). So what sort of disparity of outcomes should we expect to find between the classes in a meritocratic society, given this level of heritability of intelligence?[140]

We can work this out using Goldthorpe's original figures. Obviously, the fathers and sons in his study did not grow up in a perfectly meritocratic society, but what pattern of social mobility would Goldthorpe have found if they had?

Just 14 per cent of the fathers had professional-managerial jobs and 55 per cent were in the working class (the remainder were in intermediate positions which we can ignore to keep things simple). If Britain had been a perfect meritocracy when these fathers were growing up, they would have been recruited to their occupational class positions purely on the basis of their ability (again, to keep things simple, let's ignore 'effort'). All the fathers who made it to the middle class would therefore have been in the top 14 per cent of the ability distribution in their generation, and all the fathers who entered the working class would have been in the bottom 55 per cent of this distribution.

---

[139] Geoff Payne 'Labouring under a misapprehension: Politicians' perceptions and the realities of structural social mobility in Britain 1995-2010' In Paul Lambert et al., *Social Stratification: Trends and Processes*, Aldershot, Ashgate, 2012.

[140] What follows is based on Peter Saunders 'Might Britain be a meritocracy?' *Sociology* vol.29, 1995, 23-41

These proportions can be translated into IQ scores. The top 14 per cent of the IQ scale translates into IQ scores of 116 or above, and the bottom 55 per cent consists of scores of 102 or less. So if Britain had been a perfect meritocracy back then, all of the middle class fathers would have had an IQ of 116 or better, and none of the working class fathers would have had an IQ higher than 102.

We can make the same calculations for the sons. In the sons' generation, 27 per cent were in professional-managerial jobs while 44 per cent were in the working class. Had all the sons been recruited to their jobs purely on meritocratic criteria, the brightest 27 per cent (meaning an IQ of 109 or higher) would have ended up in the middle class and the bottom 44 per cent (IQ below 98) would have gravitated to the working class.

The question now is: what is the statistical probability of sons ending up in the same social class as their fathers if occupational placement in both generations had taken place purely on the basis of intelligence? How likely is it, for example, that middle class fathers with an IQ of 116 or more would produce sons with an IQ of 109 or more (the minimum score necessary if they were to follow in their fathers' footsteps)?

Bright parents tend to produce bright children, but not all their children will be bright. As we saw earlier, parents' and children's IQ scores only correlate at 0.5. This being the case, we can calculate that 59 per cent of children born to parents with an IQ of 116 or more would have an IQ of 109 or above. Had Goldthorpe's fathers and sons all been living under conditions of perfect meritocracy, we would therefore expect 59 per cent of the children in his study who were born to middle class fathers to have inherited sufficient intelligence to have stayed in that class.

Similar calculations can be made in respect of the other social mobility patterns. Under perfectly meritocratic conditions, sons with an IQ of 98 or less would have entered the working class. Assuming a correlation of 0.5 in IQ scores of fathers and sons, 21 per cent of those born to middle class fathers (IQ of 116 or more) would have scored this low, as would 58 per cent of those born to working class fathers (IQ 102 or less). Conversely, 18 per cent of sons born to working class fathers would have IQ scores of 109 or more, which would have been enough for them to secure middle class entry.

Table 1: A comparison of actual rates of social mobility with the rates predicted by a model of perfect meritocracy[141]

MOBILITY PATTERN	PREDICTED %	ACTUAL %
Middle class > middle class	59	59
Middle class > working class	21	15
Working class > middle class	18	16
Working class > working class	58	57

Having calculated all the predicted class destinations of children born to middle class and working class parents, we can now examine how our model of social mobility under perfect meritocracy compares with what Goldthorpe actually found. As we can see from Table 1, there is a remarkably high degree of fit. Indeed, with the sole exception of downward mobility from the middle class into the working class (where the actual rate of movement recorded by Goldthorpe is about 25 per cent less than that predicted for a perfect meritocracy), the model fits Goldthorpe's data almost exactly. The social mobility histories of the ten thousand men interviewed for

---

[141] Actual figures are taken from Goldthorpe's 1972 data coded according to his original class schema, taken from table 9.8.

Goldthorpe's study in 1972 look almost precisely like what we would have expected to find had they and their fathers been recruited to their class positions purely on the basis of their cognitive ability.

Goldthorpe's assertion that a disparity ratio as high as 4:1 could not possibly be the product of differences in average levels of intelligence between the classes is thus disproved. This is exactly the sort of ratio we would expect to find if the class recruitment of the fathers and sons in his study had been based solely on their intelligence.

This does not mean the meritocracy hypothesis has been proven, but it does mean that it is plausible even when assessed against Goldthorpe's data. Despite his belief that his findings had blown away any possibility that Britain might be meritocratic, we can see that even quite substantial differences in occupational outcomes between children born into different classes are not inconsistent with meritocratic selection. Far from being settled, the question of whether Britain is a meritocracy or not is actually wide open.[142] It is time to re-examine the evidence.

---

[142] Note that this argument holds looking forwards as well as backwards. Ability differentials not only predict what happened to Goldthorpe's sons' generation, at a time when middle class jobs were growing and upward mobility was therefore increasing, but also predict what will happen now that expansion in the size of the middle class has slowed and downward mobility is rising. The fact that relative social mobility rates appear to have remained fairly constant is significant, for if class advantages were key, we should have seen total fluidity fall (because there are now more middle class children with parents intent on preserving their privileges). The fact that downward mobility has been rising to complement the fall in upward mobility suggests some sort of 'self-balancing' mechanism is at work. The most plausible candidate is the 0.5 heritability of ability.

Truth #10

Unequal educational achievement by children from different social classes is mainly (but not wholly) explained by differences in average ability levels between them

We can begin by looking at the different rates of educational success achieved by children from different class backgrounds. Educational achievement is crucial because access to middle class jobs is often dependent on educational qualifications. So to what extent is educational attainment driven by ability differences, as against social class differences?

The Chief Executive of the Sutton Trust is in no doubt that education in Britain 'has been commandeered by the middle classes to retain their advantage from one generation to the next.' The education system, he says, is 'the vehicle through which inequality of incomes drives inequality of opportunities.' In his view, class background is therefore just as important as intelligence in shaping how children perform: 'School tests are as much a signal of how much support children receive as their natural ability.'[143]

None of this is true.

Gary Marks has reviewed and summarised a vast swathe of studies of educational attainment from Britain (and across

---

[143] Lee Elliot Major and Stephen Machin, *Social Mobility and its enemies* (op cit.), pp.11, 39 and 95

the OECD) over a long period of time.[144] He notes a correlation of 0.55 in the 1958 UK birth cohort between children's cognitive ability scores at age 11 and the highest level of educational qualification they subsequently attained. There is a correlation between IQ and overall GCSE performance of 0.7. While 58 per cent of children with average IQ scores go on to achieve five or more GCSE passes at grades A-C, 91 per cent of those with scores 1 standard deviation above the mean achieve this, compared with just 16 per cent of those with scores 1 standard deviation below the mean.[145]

In all the studies he reviews, Marks finds that cognitive ability, not social background, is the strongest influence. In the 1958 birth cohort, parental class (together with gender and parents' reading behaviour) explains only 15 per cent of the variation in children's reading achievement, and 11 per cent of their maths score, at age 11. Ability is a much more powerful predictor. Controlling for family income, class background and other background factors, the probability of a student in the top fifth of ability in the 1958 birth cohort achieving A-levels or higher was 70 percentage points greater than that of a student in the bottom fifth.

Class background does have some impact, but it is small. Cognitive test scores predict a child's educational attainment almost twice as successfully as their parents' level of education does, and their parents' social class has 'very little effect' at all.[146]

---

[144] Gary Marks, *Education, social background and cognitive ability* op cit. What follows is taken from chapters 5 through 9.

[145] Marks, *Education, social background and cognitive ability* op cit., p.72

[146] Research by Thienpont and Verleye finds standardised coefficients of 0.7 for test scores compared with 0.4 for parental education (Marks, *Education, social background and cognitive ability* op cit., pp.83-4). It is important to remember that the association of a child's attainment with its parents' level of education will in part be explained by innate ability, for parental education attainment partly reflects parental IQ, and parental IQ is partly transmitted to their children.

It is often suggested that children from poorer backgrounds under-achieve at school because of their family's economic circumstances, but Marks finds little or no evidence to support this either. In the 1958 birth cohort, early school leaving was strongly associated with low cognitive ability, and fathers' occupation and parental income had very small (and often statistically insignificant) effects once ability was taken into account. Youngsters with low reading and maths scores are five times more likely to leave school early than those with high scores. As for entry to higher education, once GCSE and A-level results are taken into account, social class background has no additional effect on the probability of university entry.

In the face of all this evidence, even John Goldthorpe has been forced to accept that ability plays some part in explaining why children from different class backgrounds differ in their average levels of educational attainment. He no longer dismisses as 'Smilesian' or 'Social Darwinist' the claim that cognitive ability varies across social classes.[147] However, he still insists ability is less important than class in shaping educational outcomes.

In a 2013 paper with Bukodi and Erikson, Goldthorpe uses UK data from the 1946, 1958 and 1970 birth cohorts to try to demonstrate the greater importance of social background. First, the authors measure the strength of association between children's educational attainment and three background variables (their parents' class, parental status and parental education). They then add a measure of the children's cognitive ability to their regression model to

---

[147] Although he does accuse Gary Marks of 'genetics evangelism', which suggests that his contemptuous labelling of people who disagree with him remains as robust as ever – E. Bukodi, M. Bourne, B. Betthauser and J. Goldthorpe, 'Reply to Gary Marks' *Research in Social Stratification and Mobility*, vol. 59, 2019.

see what difference it makes. They report that the strength of association between social background and educational attainment falls by 'only around a third' when ability is added.[148]

They claim this shows that class trumps ability in determining educational outcomes: 'The introduction of cognitive ability into the analysis does not massively diminish the effects of social origins on educational attainment. To the contrary, we would regard as particularly notable the extent to which the effects of parental class, status and education alike are maintained.'[149] But as they well know but fail to mention, the order in which variables are introduced into a regression model like this is crucial if the aim is to compare their relative explanatory strengths. Their approach skewed their results heavily in favour of the SAD hypothesis.

We know that the class position and level of education achieved by parents depends partly on how intelligent they are. We also know that parents pass a good chunk of this intelligence on to their children through their genes. This means that the parental background variables which Goldthorpe used in his model all correlate quite strongly with children's IQs. By entering these background variables into the model first, all this 'shared variance' got attributed to the parents' education and class, and none of it to the children's ability. When the child's ability was then entered into the model at a later stage, its impact was lessened because all the effect it shares with the background variables had already been measured. What Goldthorpe and his co-authors effectively did was measure the impact of children's

<hr>

[148] E. Bukodi, R. Erikson and J. Goldthorpe, 'The effects of social origins and cognitive ability on educational attainment: Evidence from Britain and Sweden' *Barnett Working Paper* 13-04, 2013, p.13

[149] E. Bukodi, R. Erikson and J. Goldthorpe, 'The effects of social origins and cognitive ability on educational attainment', op cit., p.34.

ability having first stripped out any cognitive ability they shared with their parents![150]

In a later (2018) paper with a different set of authors, Goldthorpe as good as admits this.[151] But he then proceeds to generate another skewed model. This time, using data from the 1958 and 1970 national birth cohort studies as well as a 1991/92 birth cohort study from the county of Avon, he and his co-authors develop a simple path model designed to measure both the direct effect of social background (parental class, status and education) on the educational qualifications children achieve, and the indirect effect of social background mediated by its impact on children's ability. They find that 'no more than' 50 per cent of the total effect of social background is mediated by its association with children's cognitive ability: 'We can say that at least half of the effects of social origins is direct – that is, occurs other than through early life cognitive ability.'[152]

This sounds more impressive than it actually is. It does *not* mean that half of a child's educational attainment is explained by its social background. All it means is that up to half of the impact that social background has on children's educational qualifications is due to the link between parents' attributes and the IQ of their children. This, however, begs

---

[150] Had they started out by measuring the strength of association between children's ability and their educational attainment, and then added the background variables, they would have got a very different result. At the very least, therefore, they should have run the model twice (entering the background variables followed by ability, then entering ability followed by the background variables) and reported on the different results achieved. But they didn't.

[151] He admits that his own previous work did 'not adequately accommodate the fact that cognitive ability is itself quite strongly associated with social origins' M. Bourne, E. Bukodi, B. Betthauser and J. Goldthorpe, 'Persistence of the social: The role of cognitive ability in mediating the effects of social origins on educational attainment in Britain' *Research in Social Stratification and Mobility* 2018, vol.58, p.12

[152] Bourne, et al., 'Persistence of the social', op cit., p.17

the obvious question: how much impact does a child's background have on its educational attainment, and how does this compare with the impact of its cognitive ability?

To find the answer to that, we have to dig around in an online supplement to Goldthorpe's paper, for he and his co-authors did not include these statistics in the paper itself. Fortunately, Gary Marks went looking for them. It turns out that the standardised effects of ability on qualifications in the three cohorts were 0.45, 0.32 and 0.49. These compare with the standardised effects of the combined social background variables of between 0.04 and 0.15. In all three studies, ability was thus a far more important influence on educational attainment than parental class, status and education all combined, although you would never know this from reading the paper itself.[153] The effect of ability is at least three times greater than the combined social background variables, which is precisely what we would expect given all the other research which has been done on this topic.[154]

---

[153] As Marks says, 'It is these small [background] effects that are emphasized throughout the paper as if they are larger than the effects of cognitive ability' Gary Marks, 'Socioeconomic background, education, cognitive ability and genetics: A commentary on Bourne et al' *Research in Stratification and Mobility*, vol. 59, 2019.

[154] In their latest book, Bukodi and Goldthorpe sidestep the issue of their relative importance altogether, telling us: 'Our concern is not, we should stress, with determining the importance of cognitive ability in individuals' chances of attaining [educational success] *as compared to that* of their parents' social class, status and education' (*Social mobility and education in Britain*, p.113). Rather, they say they are only interested in demonstrating that social background still has some effect over and above IQ (something nobody has ever denied). In a book of 224 pages, they therefore never address the key question of how big an effect social background has on educational success, compared with the effect of cognitive ability. Rather than acknowledging that ability is a far more powerful predictor of educational achievement than any combination of social background variables, they try to close the debate down altogether.

Truth #11

Educational attainment has a sizeable genetic component

The ability differences between children that get expressed in their varying educational achievements derive in large part from the genes they inherit from their parents.

Robert Plomin runs an ongoing UK study of sixteen thousand pairs of twins, one-third of whom are identical MZ twins who share exactly the same DNA, and two-thirds non-identical (DZ), sharing 50 per cent of their DNA. By comparing the similarity and differences of educational achievements by the MZ and DZ twins, he shows that performance across all school subjects is 'substantially heritable' (i.e. based in the genes they inherited from their parents).

Reading skills (measured by fluency and phonetics) are 'highly heritable', as is ability in learning foreign languages. Aptitude in science and maths is also substantially genetic. Across the board, performance on school attainment tests is, on average, 60 per cent heritable.[155] 'Genetics,' Plomin says, 'is by far the major source of individual differences in school

---

[155] Not surprisingly, occupational status and income are also both highly heritable (around 40 per cent, based on twins studies). The class and income we achieve in life is to a large extent determined by our DNA (Plomin, *Blueprint*, op cit., p.101). Taking account of heritability, Plomin suggests that the strength of association found in the UK between the social class of parents and the class of their children, and between the income of parents and the income of their children, is broadly consistent with the operation of 'substantially meritocratic' selection procedures in the educational and occupational systems.

achievement, even though genetics is rarely mentioned in relation to education.'[156]

He argues that this high level of heritability means there is 'substantial equality of opportunity' in the British education system (notwithstanding what the Chief Executive of the Sutton Trust might think).[157] This is because, with genes explaining so much, there is little scope left for things like parental income, parents' 'cultural capital', social contacts and networks, and all the other factors emphasised by the SAD hypothesis to explain. 'Parent-offspring resemblance for educational attainment primarily reflects genetic influence, not environmental inequality.'[158]

The evidence does not consist solely of results from twins studies. As we saw earlier, researchers have begun to identify the DNA variations which generate this high level of heritability of educational attainment. As we saw, genome-wide association (GWA) studies had by 2018 succeeded in predicting 11 to 13 per cent of the variance in educational attainment (measured crudely by years of education).[159] According to Robert Plomin, 'The educational attainment polygenic score is already among the most powerful predictors in psychology.'[160]

In an analysis of findings from five different longitudinal studies (three American, one English and one from New Zealand), Daniel Belsky and his colleagues find that individuals who rate highly on a polygenic score for educational attainment not only perform better at school (in the English study, for example, they achieved better GCSE

[156] Robert Plomin, *Blueprint*, op cit., p.88

[157] Robert Plomin, *Blueprint*, op cit., p.88

[158] Robert Plomin, *Blueprint*, op cit., p.175

[159] Lee et al, 'Gene discovery and polygenic prediction from a genome-wide association study of educational attainment in 1.1 million individuals', op cit.

[160] Robert Plomin, *Blueprint*, op cit., p.158

results, even after controlling for parents' education), but are also more likely to be upwardly mobile (again, even after controlling for parental education). Moreover, among siblings raised together by the same parents in the same households, those with the higher polygenic score achieved better school qualifications and were more likely to be upwardly mobile (confirming that the genes we inherit from our parents have an independent effect on educational and occupational outcomes).[161]

[161] Daniel Belsky et al., 'Genetic analysis of social class mobility in five longitudinal studies' *PNAS*, vol.115, 2018, E7275-E7284

Truth #12

A large number of middle class candidates entering top universities does not mean these universities are biased against working class applicants

According to the Sutton Trust, only 1 in 8 of the students at Oxford and Cambridge are from the lower band of social classes (classes 4 to 7 on the National Statistics social class schema, covering small business and self-employed, lower technical and supervisory, semi-routine and routine work). As many as half of the students at the lowest-ranked UK universities come from these lower class backgrounds, but children from these classes struggle to gain entry to the top institutions. Middle class students are three times more likely than working class students to be at 'high status' universities.[162]

Can these differences be explained by differences in cognitive ability levels between the classes? Or are our top universities discriminating against working class and lower middle class applicants?

The Sutton Trust acknowledges that 73 per cent of the 'class gap' in university recruitment is explained by students' 'prior academic achievement.' In other words, middle class students tend to have better A-level grades than working class students, which is why they get more offers from top universities. What the report doesn't say,

---

[162] John Jerrim, *Family background and access to high status universities* Sutton Trust, 2013

however, is that this is largely because they are, on average, more intelligent.[163]

In a pure meritocracy, the top universities will aim to recruit the brightest students, regardless of their social class background. Given that intelligence varies by social class and is 50 per cent heritable, this means children born to successful, middle class parents will achieve greater success in gaining entry to top universities than children born to working class parents. But should the disparity between them be this great?

Bruce Charlton, an evolutionary psychologist at Newcastle University, tried to answer this in a 2008 article.[164] With almost half of young people getting to university, he reasoned that a meritocratic selection system would recruit the top half of the ability distribution (i.e. those with an IQ of 100 or more) for some sort of university entry. Of these, about one in six would get accepted by an established, high-reputation university – defined by Charlton as one of the 'redbrick' universities. Translated into approximate IQ scores, this would require an IQ of 115 or more (one standard

---

[163] Unfortunately, the report does not have any information on the average IQ scores of youngsters from different classes who end up in different universities, but it does note that our best universities require students to have 'advanced cognitive skills' which many working class youngsters lack. Those from homes in the lowest quintile of the occupational status ladder, for example, perform much worse than those from homes in the highest quintile on standardised tests like the PISA reading assessment (17 per cent of the latter achieve level 5, compared with only 3 per cent of the former). The report notes that a similar attainment gap between social classes is found in all countries. In Sweden, for example, the gap is 19 per cent against 4 per cent; in the Netherlands, 17 per cent against 4 per cent; in Canada, 27 per cent against 7 per cent; and so on. Given that reading skills have been found to be highly heritable, it seems likely that most of these differences are due to innate ability variations between the classes in all these countries, including the UK.

[164] Bruce Charlton, 'Social class differences in IQ: Implications for the government's "fair access" political agenda' *Times Higher Education* 23 May 2008

deviation above the mean). Meanwhile, if Oxbridge is assumed to limit its intake to the top 2 per cent or so of the cohort, it would require an IQ equivalent to 130 or more (2 standard deviations above the mean) to get in there.

Charlton then drew on research documenting the average IQ levels of people in different social classes. The average IQ of unskilled workers is around 90, while that of the highest occupational class (senior professional and managerial workers) is around 115.[165] Given 50 per cent heritability of intelligence, he calculated the probability of children from each social class born to parents with the average IQ level for that class being bright enough to qualify for different levels of university entry. The results are startling.

For children born to unskilled worker parents with an IQ of 90, there is a 25 per cent chance of having an IQ of 100 (high enough to qualify for a low-status university), a 5 per cent chance of having an IQ of 115 (high enough to get into a good redbrick university), and just a 0.5 chance of having an IQ of 130 (good enough to get you into Oxford or Cambridge). On these calculations, the reason why Oxbridge recruits relatively few students from the lowest social class is that only 1 in 200 of them are bright enough to go there.

Compare these figures with those for children born to senior professional and managerial worker families where parental IQ averages 115. With an IQ that high, we can expect 84 per cent of children to qualify for entry to any university (IQ required: 100); 50 per cent to qualify for a redbrick university (IQ required: 115); and 16 per cent to meet the level needed for Oxbridge (IQ required: 130).

---

[165] He uses the material summarised and reviewed in Michael Argyle, *The Psychology of Social Class* Routledge, 1994

Charlton concluded that children born to the highest social class parents are 3 times more likely to have the ability needed to go to any university, 10 times more likely to be bright enough to get into a good university, and 32 times more likely to be bright enough for Oxford or Cambridge. As he put it: 'With a fully meritocratic admissions policy we should expect to see a differential in favour of the highest social classes relative to the lowest social classes at all universities, and this differential would become very large at a highly-selective university such as Oxford or Cambridge.'

This is not the sort of thing educationalists or politicians wanted to hear. When Charlton published his calculations, the National Union of Students dismissed his work as 'wrong-headed, irresponsible and insulting.' The University and College Union claimed his findings showed only that 'people who enjoy a more privileged upbringing have a better start in life' (precisely the opposite of what his findings had actually shown). And the then Minister for Higher Education, Bill Rammell, accused Charlton of suggesting that 'people should know their place.'[166] None of his critics addressed his data, nor his analysis; they simply refused to engage with it, preferring instead to attack his motives and character. Yet his logic was watertight, and his calculations have since been reinforced by findings in behavioural genetics.

Noting that graduate parents often produce children who also go to university, Robert Plomin denies that this can be explained by the cultural head-start they get while growing up. He insists it is DNA differences that are driving it.

It's not just that youngsters who get to university have higher polygenic scores for educational attainment than

---

[166] Polly Curtis, 'Student Union rejects academic's IQ claims' *The Guardian* 22 May 2008

those who don't, but that 'upwardly mobile children' (those attending university whose parents did not go to university) have higher scores than their peers who are not upwardly mobile, and 'downwardly mobile children' (who do not get to university even though their parents did) have lower polygenic scores. Genetics, Plomin says, accounts for half the individual differences in university entry: 'Parent-offspring resemblance for educational attainment primarily reflects genetic influence, not environmental inequality.'[167]

Far from discriminating against working class candidates, our top universities have for some time been admitting poorer students on lower grades than those from more privileged backgrounds. Analysis of the school records of half a million youngsters born in 1991/92 shows that, although few of those from the most deprived backgrounds made it into top universities (under 3 per cent of those claiming free school meals, compared with 10 per cent of all others), those who did gain entry got there with significantly poorer average GCSE and A-level results.[168] Only 75 per cent of them had five good GCSE passes in core subjects, compared with 95 per cent of those who had never claimed free school meals; 47 per cent had at least three A-level passes at grade B or above, compared with 73 per cent of the others. Even the very best universities (Oxbridge, UCL and Imperial) revealed the same bias. Far from discriminating against lower class and socially disadvantaged applicants, therefore, it seems our top universities have been discriminating in favour of them, and by a significant margin.

---

[167] Plomin, *Blueprint*, op cit., p.175
[168] Claire Crawford, Lindsey MacMillan, Anna Vignoles, *Progress made by high-attaining children from disadvantaged backgrounds* op cit.

Truth #13

Top universities are not biased in favour of applicants from private schools (if anything, the reverse may be true)

It is repeatedly argued by politicians (as well as by quangos like the Social Mobility Commission and think-tanks like the Sutton Trust) that Britain's top universities unfairly favour applicants from independent, fee-paying schools. The evidence cited for this claim is that only 7 per cent of British children attend private schools, but they account for 23 per cent of young people entering Russell Group universities, and for 42% of those going to Oxbridge.[169] Citing these figures, the Labour Party has recently committed to limiting the number of privately-educated students admitted to Oxford and Cambridge to a maximum of 7 per cent.[170]

The Tories also regularly use this 7 per cent figure to attack what they see as unfair private school privilege. In her speech in Derby in 2018, the then Prime Minister Theresa May said: 'Almost a quarter of the students at our

---

[169] See, for example, Social Mobility Commission, *State of the Nation* 2018-19, op cit., p.53; Sutton Trust, cited by Sean Coughlin, 'Oxbridge over-recruits from eight schools' *BBC News* 7 December 2018, https://www.bbc.co.uk/news/education-46470838; Damian Hinds speech to Resolution Foundation, 31 July 2018 www.gov.uk/government/speeches/education-secretary-sets-vision-for-boosting-social-mobility

[170] 'The @AbolishEton campaign succeeded in having a motion passed at the 2019 Labour Party conference to stop universities such as Oxford and Cambridge admitting more than 7% of private school students. See Sian Griffiths, 'Labour vows to end "burning injustice" of private schools', *The Times*, 21 July 2019

research-intensive universities come from the 7% of the population who go to private school. And the professions which draw their recruits primarily from these institutions remain unrepresentative of the country as a whole, skewed in favour of a particular social class. For the boy from a working class home here in Derby, the odds are stacked against him.'[171]

But it's not true.

It is again Bruce Charlton who has pointed out the fallacy in the argument that, since only 7 per cent of children attend private schools, they should account for only 7 per cent of students at top universities.[172] The key statistic, he says, is the number of A-level students studying in private schools, for A-level students constitute the pool from which universities are selecting.

It turns out that about one-sixth of A-level students are in the independent sector.[173] Even if we assume that the ability level of these students is no higher than that of students in the state sector, we should therefore expect youngsters educated in the private sector to account for at least one-sixth of entrants to the top universities – not one-fourteenth, as the Social Mobility Commission, the Labour Party and Mrs. May all suggest.

But Charlton goes further. He points out that private schools select their intake (at least to some extent) by ability, whereas the vast majority of state schools do not. It follows

---

[171] Theresa May, *The right education for everyone* Speech delivered in Derby, 19 February 2018 www.gov.uk/government/speeches/pm-the-right-education-for-everyone

[172] Bruce Charlton, *Proportion of private school kids applying to college is about 18%, not 7%* 14 July 2010 https://charltonteaching.blogspot.com/20/10/17/proportion-of-private-school-kids.html

[173] Charlton estimates the proportion at 18%. More recently, Toby Young has given a figure of 16 per cent ('Britain is becoming more meritocratic, not less' *The Spectator*, 29 June 2019).

that the average ability level in the independent schools must be higher than in the state sector, which means we should expect their alumni to be over-represented in the best universities (assuming the best universities are selecting on meritocratic criteria). Taking the effects of academic selection into account, Charlton speculates that the private/state school entry rates into both Russell Group universities and Oxbridge colleges probably reflects the average ability distributions in the two sectors.

Predictably, Charlton's work provoked outrage among academics and policy wonks (he notes ruefully that 'these facts and statistics are clearly unpopular in some quarters).'[174] Yet his reasoning has (again) subsequently been borne out by research in behavioural genetics. Robert Plomin reports, for example, that children in private schools have 'substantially higher educational attainment polygenic scores' than those in state comprehensives.[175] Their DNA shows they are on average more intelligent.

There is also another factor that Charlton does not mention. Private schools tend to develop the potential of their students more successfully than the state sector does. In my research with Rod Bond on the 1958 birth cohort, we found that, controlling for IQ, those attending private school at 16 gain better qualifications than those attending state schools. This effect is modest but significant, and it mainly

---

[174] Bruce Charlton, 'Social class and IQ' *Mensa magazine*, December 2008. The reason we would expect an even higher proportion of private school students to make it into Oxbridge than into the Russell Group universities has to do with the properties of the normal distribution curve. If the average IQ in private schools is higher than in state schools, then the number of students at the very highest end of the IQ distribution (say, 2 or more standard deviations above the mean) will be much higher – and it is from this extreme end of the distribution that the very top universities will recruit.

[175] Plomin, *Blueprint*, op cit., pp.172-3

reflects the raised level of motivation displayed by students in the independent sector.[176]

Mainly because they are on average brighter, but also partly because they are generally more motivated, children at private schools thus out-perform children at state schools in achieving the qualifications necessary to get into a good university. They may only account for 16 per cent of those sitting A-levels, but between them, independent school pupils make up 32 per cent of all A-level candidates who achieve three A grades or better (the sorts of grades normally required to get an offer from Oxford or Cambridge).[177] Indeed, almost half (48%) of all the A levels achieved by independent school pupils in 2017 were at grade A or A*, compared with 'only' 26 per cent nationally. Even when we control for the social class origins of the students, those from private schools still outperformed state school pupils by 8 per cent.[178] They got better A-level results, which is why more of them got into top universities.

If there is a 'private school bias' in university entry, it is running in the opposite direction from that imagined by Mrs. May and the Labour Party. In 2016-17, 25 per cent of pupils gaining 3 A grades or better at A-level were in private

---

[176] Rod Bond and Peter Saunders 'Routes of success' *British Journal of Sociology*, vol.50, 1999, p.239. Interestingly, Plomin suggests that private schools add little to the potential that their students already have, arguing that they select on the basis of cognitive tests which fully predict their later achievements in GCSE examinations. Against this, even critics accept that independent schools get more from their pupils due to their 'respect [for] the need for a disciplined environment for learning' and the attention they give to 'generating a positive and therefore motivating experience' (Francis Green and David Kynaston, 'Britain's private school problem' *The Guardian* 13 January 2019).

[177] Social Mobility Commission, *Elitist Britain?* 2014, p.16. The University of Oxford notes that 28.4% of independent school candidates get AAA+ grades compared with 6.6% of state school candidates – *Access and Participation Plan* 2019-20, p.5

[178] Social Mobility Commission, *State of the Nation* 2018-19, op cit., p.54

schools, but only 23% of young people entering Russell Group universities that year were from private schools.[179] Judging by these figures, applicants from private schools appear to be slightly *under-represented* in the 'research-intensive universities' which Mrs. May was so concerned about.

As we shall see in the final section of this essay, this under-representation is likely to increase, the more the government pressurises our top universities into taking fewer students from the independent sector. Little wonder some private school heads have recently begun to complain about unfair treatment by universities of applications from their pupils.[180]

---

[179] Damian Hinds speech to Resolution Foundation, 31 July 2018, op cit.
[180] Nicola Woodcock, 'Private woe over rise of state pupils at Oxbridge' *The Times*, 11 May 2019

Truth #14

Ability and motivation far outweigh class background in predicting social class destinations in adulthood

Let us now turn from education to jobs. It's not just educational success that is driven by differences in ability between the classes. This is true of success in the competition for jobs as well.

All the children in the 1958 birth cohort study sat a general ability test at 11. The results were modestly associated with the social class from which the children were drawn (middle class children tended to perform better, r=0.24) but were more strongly associated with the social class in which they ended up at age 33 (r=0.37).[181] This is consistent with what we would expect to happen in a meritocratic system. If ability test scores were merely a reflection of class privilege, the two correlations should be the same strength. The fact that they are not shows these children were to some extent being selected for later social class entry on the basis of their ability, independently of their class origin.

The bright children in this birth cohort study almost all succeeded later in life, no matter where they started out from. Of those in the top quartile of ability scores in the test at age 11, only 5 per cent ended up in semi- or unskilled routine worker jobs, and 65 per cent made it into professional or managerial careers. The reverse, however, was not the case

---

[181] Peter Saunders, 'Social mobility in Britain: An empirical evaluation of two competing explanations' *Sociology*, vol.31, 1997, 261-288

– low ability did not necessarily mean occupational failure. Two out of five middle class children in the lowest ability quartile still made it into the middle class, as did one out of five working class children in the lowest ability quartile.

Controlling for ability differences, the chance of a middle class child, relative to a working class child, getting a middle class job fell from a disparity ratio of 2.2:1 to 1.7:1, and the risk of a working class child, relative to a middle class child, ending up in a working class job fell from a disparity ratio of 3.5:1 to 2.3:1. In other words, ability accounted for about half of the difference in occupational outcomes between children from professional-managerial backgrounds and those from semi-skilled/unskilled working class homes.

Meritocracy, of course, rewards effort as well as ability. At age 16, all the youngsters in this study completed a set of attitude questions, and their answers were combined into a scale measuring their degree of motivation at school. We also have a record of their truancy and absenteeism at school, and a measure of their attitudes to work at age 23. These rough-and-ready indicators can be included in statistical modelling together with their ability test scores to provide measures of 'merit' that cover 'effort' as well as 'ability.'

The strength of association between these merit variables and the eventual class destinations achieved by these children can be compared with the impact of various measures of social advantage and disadvantage (deriving from the SAD hypothesis). These include their parents' social class, their parents' education level,[182] their parents'

---

[182] Bukodi and Goldthorpe make great play of the importance of including parental education as well as parental class in measures of social advantage, suggesting their impact is cumulative (*Social mobility and education in Britain*, p.109). In the model developed here, I go much further by also including further measures like parental aspirations and support.

aspirations for them, the parental help and support they received (e.g. whether their parents read to them when they were young, or attended parents' evenings at their schools), their access to pre-school education and private schooling, and conditions in the home (e.g. overcrowding or lack of basic amenities) when they were growing up.

A least-squares multiple regression model predicting the occupational status this cohort achieved at age 33 shows that while their class background did play some part in shaping their class destinations, their ability and effort were far more important.[183] The effect of their ability test score at age 11 on the occupational status they achieved by age 33 was twice as strong as their level of motivation at school, and was three times stronger than their parents' social class.

John Goldthorpe refused to accept these results when I published them. Instead, in a joint article with Richard Breen, he accused me of incompetence, bias and ignorance.[184] The

---

[183] With just 22% of variance accounted for, this is not a strong model overall. A second regression model including exam passes at 16, further qualifications, and the social class of the first job after leaving school raises this to 32%. In this second model, the three newly entered variables have the biggest impact. The only variable which still has a strong independent effect on occupational outcomes at age 33 after they are added is ability. This means that ability has an impact on outcomes over and above its obvious association with formal qualifications (something Bukodi and Goldthorpe also report – *Social mobility and education in Britain*, pp. 145-6 and 149). Both models are fully set out in Peter Saunders, *Social Mobility Myths*, Civitas 2010.

[184] R. Breen and J. Goldthorpe, 'Class inequality and meritocracy: A critique of Saunders and an alternative analysis,' *British Journal of Sociology* 50,1999, 1-27. They complained that I 'disregard a large body of relevant literature' (p.6), I should have been 'better acquainted with obviously relevant literature' (p.8), I need to 're-read' the literature on IQ (footnote 10); and my 'disregard' of earlier studies 'is conspicuous (footnote 21). They also question my methodological competence: I do not 'securely grasp the "logic" of odds ratios' (p.5); I 'ignore' the complexity in interpreting regression models (p.7); I 'introduced biases' in my measures to favour my own position (p.21); I use 'undesirable' and 'ad hoc' procedures for dealing with missing cases (footnote 9); and my methodology is 'biased' (p.8). For a detailed rebuttal of these charges, see *Social Mobility Myths*, chapter 6, and Peter Saunders, 'Reflections on the meritocracy debate in Britain' *British Journal of Sociology*, vol.53, 2002, 559-74.

essence of his complaint was that I should have used his model of social classes (rather than the official government model at the time), that I should have adopted his preferred measures of ability and motivation, and that I should have applied his recommended method of analysing the data.

So I re-ran my original models to comply with Goldthorpe's preferences. Indeed, this time around I deliberately maximised the potential explanatory power of the class background measures and minimised the potential impact of the merit variables to give his SAD hypothesis the greatest possible explanatory advantage.[185]

The result was a model where the impact on class destinations of people's ability and motivation still far outweighed that of any of the other variables. Parents' level of education was statistically significant, as were class origins – but only if the father was in a professional-managerial occupation or was a self-employed small businessman (suggesting that class origins have their main effect through the ability of middle-class parents to prevent their children from sliding downwards, but not through any 'barriers' to working class advancement). Knowing whether or not somebody had been born into a working class household *did not help at all* in predicting where they ended up at age 33.

---

[185] The original regression model was developed in an exploratory 'stepwise' manner, allowing the order in which variables were entered to be determined by the strength of their association with the dependent variable. This is standard procedure. Because ability scores correlated with class destination more strongly than class of origin did, ability was entered before class. As we saw earlier, however, variables entered first in a multiple regression can appear stronger than they really are, for they claim all the variance that they may share with other variables which are not entered until later. To ensure that the SAD hypothesis got all the help I could possibly give it, I therefore ran the model again, this time forcing the weaker SAD variables to enter the model first so they could soak up all available shared variance (a procedure which Goldthorpe has himself used, as we saw earlier).

Even with class origins defined and measured as Goldthorpe wanted them to be, they explained at most just 7 per cent of the variance in occupational destinations at age 33. Adding other measures of social advantage or disadvantage raised this to 10 per cent. Only then did I add the ability test scores at age 11 and motivation at age 16 to the model (thus minimising their possible explanatory power). The total proportion of variance explained by the model immediately doubled to 19 per cent, and when qualifications were added, it was further raised to 27 per cent.[186] I ended up with a model where class origins accounted at most for a quarter of the explained variance in class destinations, while ability and motivation accounted for *at least* one-third – and this after deliberately biasing the model in favour of the SAD hypothesis.

The best test of the reliability of any social scientific finding is whether the same result is reproduced by different researchers working independently of each other on different data sets. And in this case, it has been.

In complete ignorance of my debate with Goldthorpe, David Nettle, from the Open University's Department of Psychology and Biological Sciences, published a paper in 2003 investigating the importance of cognitive ability in influencing class mobility among members of the 1958 birth cohort when they reached 42 years of age (nine years on from when I had studied them).[187] Using a five-class schema, he found that 60 per cent of the men in the sample now occupied a different class position from the one their fathers occupied, and the correlation between class of origin

---

[186] The full regression model explained 32% of the variance, the same as my earlier regression model

[187] David Nettle, 'Intelligence and class mobility in the British population' *British Journal of Psychology* vol.94, 2003, 551-61

and class of destination was just 0.26. Cognitive ability, measured by their ability test scores at age 11, was still the key factor explaining upward and downward mobility. After taking test scores into account, the correlation between fathers' and sons' class locations fell to just 0.16. Nettle concluded: 'Intelligence is the strongest single factor causing class mobility in contemporary societies that has been identified.'[188]

Nettle's is not the only study to corroborate my findings. Leon Feinstein looked at the relative significance of class background and cognitive ability for the earnings, qualifications and risk of unemployment of the 1970 birth cohort by the time they reached age 26.[189] He found that reading and maths scores at age 10 were the best predictor of qualifications achieved by age 26, that fathers' class was not statistically significant, and that ability (measured by the age 10 scores) had an additional effect on earnings, over and above its link to qualifications. Bright people, in other words, tend to earn more, even after their superior qualifications are taken into account (which is exactly what I found for the 1958 cohort).

Sophie von Stumm and her colleagues also investigated the 1970 birth cohort, but she focused on males when they reached the age of 30. She found that 'intelligence predicted class attainments to a far greater extent than social class of origin.'[190]

---

[188] David Nettle, 'Intelligence and class mobility in the British population', op cit., p.560

[189] Leon Feinstein, 'The relative economic importance of academic, psychological and behavioural attributes developed in childhood' London School of Economics *Centre for Economic Performance Papers*, no.443, 2000

[190] Sophie von Stumm, Catherine Gale, G. David Batty, Ian Deary, 'Childhood intelligence, locus of control and behaviour disturbance as determinants of intergenerational social mobility' *Intelligence* vol.37, 2009, p.327

Working with a different set of researchers, von Stumm also analysed the class destinations achieved by a sample of twelve thousand Aberdeen boys born in the years 1950-1956 who completed four mental ability tests when they were 11 years of age. They were followed up when they were aged between 46 and 51. A path model was constructed which accounted for 48% of the variance in class destinations – a strong model – and again, intelligence was the key explanatory variable. The ability test scores of these boys were twice as strong as their social class origins in predicting their educational achievements, and were almost twice as strong in predicting their class position in middle age.

There are now literally dozens of studies which show that IQ is the key influence on people's educational and occupational attainment, that it is to a significant extent inherited from their parents, and that it is much more important than their class origins are.[191] This does not mean that intelligence is the sole explanation for where people end up in life, but it does mean that it's certainly a bigger influence than class background.

---

[191] This is true in other countries too. A 'meta-analysis' conducted by Tarmo Strenze includes 49 different longitudinal studies from around the world and finds that 'intelligence is a better predictor of success' than either parental class or qualifications 'Intelligence and socioeconomic success' *Intelligence* vol.35, 2007, p.415

Truth #15

Once qualifications, cognitive ability and motivation are taken into account, class origins play only an indirect role in influencing class destinations

Building on my work on the 1958 birth cohort work, Rod Bond and I later developed a richer and more sophisticated 'path model' using structural linear equations (Fig.3).[192]

We analysed the life trajectories of more than four thousand men in the 1958 data set, inspecting about eighty different variables, each of which could in theory have influenced their occupational outcomes at age 33. Our aim was not only to measure the relative contribution made by each of these variables, but also to trace the way they interacted with one another. In this way, we were able to determine *how* different aspects of people's lives impact on their eventual class destinations – whether, for example, they directly affect the jobs people end up in or have an effect only through their interaction with other things in their background.

We included various measures of these men's social class background (the social class of their grandparents as well as their father's and mother's class at different points in their childhood), their father's and mother's level of education, the types of primary and secondary school they attended (state or private), and conditions in their home (specifically,

---

[192] Rod Bond and Peter Saunders 'Routes of success' *British Journal of Sociology*, vol.50, 1999. The model was limited to males.

whether they grew up in overcrowded housing). We also included measures of how much support they received from their parents while they were growing up – whether they had been encouraged to stay on at school, what kind of employment their parents hoped they would go into, whether their parents took an active interest in their schooling (e.g. by attending parents' evenings), and whether teachers regarded their parents as supportive. Finally, we looked at various measures of their cognitive ability (their score on the ability test at age 11, plus literacy and numeracy test scores at 7 and 16), their levels of ambition and motivation at various ages, and the formal qualifications they achieved at school and in their subsequent training and careers.

Once all the interaction effects were taken into account, any variables which had no significant direct or indirect influence on occupational status at age 33 were dropped from the model. Of those that remained, some (those in rectangular boxes in Fig.3) were directly measured in the various sweeps of the survey, while others (shown in circles) were estimated from a combination of directly-observed measures (so-called 'latent variables').[193]

The question we asked was: how do all these variables impact on each other, and which ones are key in determining the occupational status people achieve as adults? The resulting path diagram is shown in Figure 3. Whenever a variable was found to have a significant impact on another variable, this is shown by an arrowed line running between them. The strength of this impact (having taken account of the influence of any other variables that are also associated

---

[193] For example, 'crowded accommodation' was directly measured at ages 7, 11 and 16 by asking about the number of rooms per person living in the house at that time; 'parental interest', by contrast, was a latent variable constructed at ages 7, 11 and 16 from three sets of information gathered from the survey (mother's level of interest in the child's schooling, father's level of interest, and a measure of how often parents had contact with the school).

with it) is measured by the coefficients in small boxes on each line.

Tracing the arrows leading to occupational status at age 33, it can be seen that only four of the measures in our model had a *direct* effect on occupational attainment – qualifications gained from secondary education, additional qualifications gained after leaving school, motivation at school at age 16, and academic ability at age 11. Social class background and parental support and encouragement had some *indirect* influence on the status of the jobs people ended up with, but only because they were related to their ability score and level of motivation when they were at school.

This is important because it means there is nothing else about their class background (e.g. their accent or their parents' social networks) that significantly affected children's achievements. If factors like these had been important, this would have shown up as a direct path from parental class to occupational status achieved at age 33. The fact that there is no direct path shows the model has not omitted anything significant about their social class background.

Table 2 summarises how much of a contribution (direct and indirect) each of the variables in the model made to explaining occupational status at age 33. Taken as a whole, the model explains 35 per cent of the variance in occupational status (so there are a lot of things influencing people's class destinations that we cannot predict or measure, even starting out with 80 different variables). But looking at the variance that we can explain, it is clear that one single variable ended up accounting for *fully half* of it. That variable was individuals' ability test scores at age 11.[194]

---

[194] Interestingly, it is ability at age 11 rather than at age 16 which has a direct effect on occupational status at age 33. Measures of ability at age 11 included a test of general ability and teacher ratings, as well as reading and maths tests, whereas at age 16, only maths and reading test scores were used. The measures at age 11 therefore explicitly included IQ, and it is this that is doing the heavy lifting.

Figure 3: Path Model predicting Occupational Status of males in the 1958 Birth Cohort at age 33. (A larger version of this chart is available at http://www.civitas.org.uk/content/files/SaundersFig3PathModel.pdf)

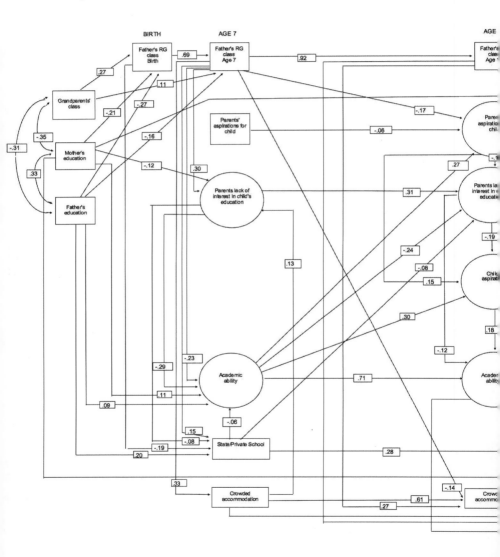

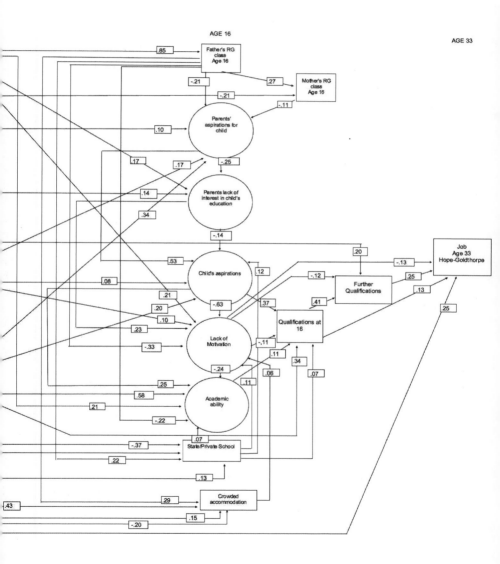

Table 2: Proportion of variance in occupational prestige at age 33 explained by different clusters of variables

VARIABLE	PROPORTION OF VARIANCE EXPLAINED
Social advantages/disadvantages:	
Parents' class	0.03
Housing conditions	0.00*
Private/state schooling	0.00*
Parents' behaviour/attitudes:	
Aspirations for child	0.01
Interest in child's education	0.03
Individual characteristics:	
Cognitive ability	0.17
Ambition (motivation)	0.05
Qualifications	
Post-16 qualifications	0.06
TOTAL VARIANCE EXPLAINED	0.35

*Less than 0.01

The effect of cognitive ability at age 11 was both direct and indirect – it influenced the level of qualifications people achieved (and through these qualifications indirectly influenced the kinds of jobs they got into), but it also had a direct effect on occupational success over and above its link to qualifications. This means not only that bright people tend to become better qualified and therefore get higher status jobs, but also that later in life, even if they are competing for jobs or promotions with other people who have the same level of qualifications that they have, they are likely to out-perform them.[195]

A high level of motivation and aspiration (what we called 'ambition') was also an important influence on where people ended up. This is a rough approximation of the element of 'effort' in Michael Young's definition of meritocracy as 'ability plus effort.' Ambition and ability each had independent effects on occupational achievement, as well as affecting each other (being bright tends to encourage children to raise their aspirations, and those with ambition subsequently do better in tests – it's a virtuous circle). Table 2 tells us that while ability accounted for half of the explained variance in occupational status at age 33 (17 per cent of the total variance), ambition explained another 15 per cent of it (5 per cent of the total).

People's social class backgrounds, by contrast, accounted for just 8 per cent of the explained variance (3 per cent of the total). Parents' social class, parents' level of education, housing conditions and private or state schooling all had some impact on the jobs people ended up in at age 33, but their influence was only indirect, and it was very modest overall. When direct and indirect effects were added

---

[195] The fact that ability has a continuing effect throughout people's careers, over and above their formal qualifications, is further strong evidence of the importance of meritocratic selection in the labour market. Oddly, though, Bukodi and Goldthorpe suggest the meritocracy thesis is *weakened* by such evidence! Noting that 'the effect of individuals' ability in shaping their class histories would by no means appear to be fully expressed via their educational attainment at labour market entry', they conclude that 'an education-based meritocracy has still some way to go' (*Social mobility and education in Britain*, pp.145-6). Following this logic, a meritocracy should reward only that element of an individual's ability which is captured in the formal qualifications they acquire – if bright people continue to get rewarded for showing initiative and originality, this is a sign that the education system must have failed to recognise their talents properly. The argument makes no sense.

together, ability, measured at age 11, was between five and six times stronger than the effect of these socio-economic factors.

This path model clearly reinforces my earlier arguments. If you want to know why some individuals achieve a higher occupational grade than others, their class background is a small part of the explanation (but only in so far as it has some influence on ability and motivation). Good parenting also helps (but again, only because it strengthens ability and motivation).[196] But the key is the individuals' own ability and motivation.

Insofar as we can explain it at all (and as is often the case in social science, much is left unexplained given that this path model only explains 35 per cent of the total variance), individual success and failure appears to be the result of individuals' own characteristics and attributes – their motivation, their pursuit of qualifications and, above all, their ability. These cannot be explained away as class background effects. The major influences on occupational destinies are, as the meritocracy thesis suggests, individual talent, hard work, and the determination to succeed.

---

[196] It is possible that at least part of the effect of parenting variables is actually due to genes shared between parents and their children, rather than the home environment. Supportive and aspirational parents probably pass on ambition to their children through their DNA as much as through tiger parenting styles.

Truth #16

Although it is the single most powerful influence on class destinations, most research on social mobility in Britain continues either to ignore ability, or to downplay it

We have seen compelling evidence that in Britain, average cognitive ability levels vary across social classes, ability is to a significant degree inherited by children from their parents, and ability, as measured by IQ tests, is the most important single factor influencing the social class position in which people end up.

Little of this has registered, however, among those driving the social mobility policy agenda in Britain. Very few government or parliamentary reports on social mobility published over the last twenty years even mention cognitive ability, still less analyse how significant it might be in shaping educational and occupational outcomes.[197] In the 150 pages of its 2019 State of the Nation report, the Social

---

[197] For fuller discussion, see Peter Saunders, *Social Mobility Delusions* (Civitas 2012), pp.16-17. One exception is the Social Mobility Commission's 2009 report, *Unleashing Aspiration: The Final Report of the Panel on Fair Access to the Professions* (Social Mobility Commission, 2009) which devotes half a page to an explanation of why it regards ability as relatively unimportant (basically, it is unconvinced that ability is genetically transmitted, it thinks disparities are too great to be explained solely by ability, and it chooses to accept Goldthorpe and Breen's spurious claim that class background has a statistically greater impact than ability on class destinations). The Commission's logic in this report appears to be that because ability does not explain everything, it can safely be ignored ('We reject the notion that the disparities observed in who gets into top careers are a product *purely* of inherited intelligence' – page 43). But nobody ever claimed these disparities are purely a product of IQ.

Mobility Commission never once mentions it.[198] This seems an extraordinary oversight, but it is no accident.

A dominant ideology has settled over the entire debate about social mobility in this country which refuses to countenance even the possibility that children born into different social classes might differ in their average ability levels. Indeed, the reverse is commonly asserted to be the case, even in the face of all the evidence to the contrary.

Former Social Mobility Commission chairman, Alan Milburn, stated back in 2009, for example, that, 'It is not ability that is unevenly distributed in our society. It is opportunity.'[199] Ten years later, Conservative government Education Secretary, Damian Hinds, was still repeating the same mantra: 'Whilst potential and talent is evenly spread, the opportunities to make the most of it sometimes aren't.'[200] But these statements are simply untrue. Ability is 'unevenly distributed in our society'; potential and talent is not 'evenly spread.'

Why is officialdom so wilfully blind to this? One of the problems is that Marxist thinking has been seeping from academic sociology into mainstream public policy discourse without many politicians even realising it. This has distorted the way the social mobility agenda has been constructed. In particular, the ideas of prominent French sociologist, Pierre Bourdieu, who dismisses the concept of intelligence as an *ideology of giftedness,'* are now mainstream within public policy circles.

For Bourdieu, 'intelligence' is nothing but an ideology used to legitimate oppression in capitalist societies. What he calls the 'ideology of giftedness' keeps 'under-privileged

---

[198] *State of the Nation 2018-19*, op cit.
[199] Foreword to *Unleashing Aspiration*, op cit., p.7
[200] Quoted in Sean Coughlin, 'Oxbridge over-recruits from eight schools' BBC News, op cit.

classes in the role which society has given them by making them see as natural inability things which are only a result of an inferior social status.'[201]

Empirically, this is complete nonsense, yet this stuff is now cited approvingly in official reports from the government's own Social Mobility Commission. For example: 'Our understanding of these processes has been significantly enhanced by the work of French sociologist Bourdieu... Scholars working in this tradition underline that merit (and hence talent) is not an objective concept but rather rooted in a system of values which are permeated by assumptions about class.'[202]

It is disturbing (to say the least) that a well-funded government body charged with objectively investigating social mobility should endorse the work of a French Marxist who thinks that differences of cognitive ability are an ideological invention of the capitalist ruling class.

Many sociologists use Bourdieu to justify their refusal even to consider the importance of intelligence, genes and IQ. In their 2019 study of social mobility in the professions, for example, Friedman and Laurison (two academics at the London School of Economics) dismiss as 'extreme', 'provocative' and 'highly dubious' the proposition that average ability varies across social classes. Never mind all the empirical evidence dating back as far as the 1960s showing that it does;[203] Bourdieu says this just an ideology,

---

[201] P. Bourdieu, 'The school as a conservative force' in J. Eggleston (ed), *Contemporary Research in the Sociology of Education* (London, Methuen, 1974), p.42.

[202] Louise Ashley et al, *A qualitative evaluation of non-educational barriers to the elite professions* Social Mobility Commission, June 2015, p.26

[203] For example: Bruce Eckland, 'Ability, Education, and Occupational Mobility', *American Sociological Review*, vol. 30, 1965, pp. 735-746; Bruce Eckland, 'Genetics and Sociology: A Reconsideration', *American Sociological Review*, vol.32, 1967, pp. 173-194.

and that's a good enough excuse for them to dismiss it. So confident are these two in rejecting the existence of class-based cognitive ability differences that they readily admit that even if they had IQ data for the subjects of their study (which they don't), they would refuse to use it![204]

Given this sort of ideological blindness, it is not surprising that intelligence (measured by IQ tests) is so rarely included in academic research (and hence gets ruled out of social policy debates too).[205] And even when it is included, it is often analysed in such a way as to minimise its explanatory impact.

We have seen that in his early work, John Goldthorpe was as dismissive as anyone of the notion that ability differences might explain the pattern of social mobility he had discovered. More recently, though, he has responded to the growing mountain of evidence that differential ability can explain much of the difference in class outcomes by shifting his initial position. But he hasn't shifted very far.

He now accepts that cognitive ability does have some impact on social class destinations, but he still insists that class-of-origin advantages and disadvantages are more important. To support this implausible claim, he dismisses out of hand regression modelling showing the explanatory power of SAD variables to be much weaker than that of

---

[204] 'We may not be able to measure something like IQ – or indeed wish to…' Friedman and Laurison, *The class ceiling*, op cit., location 1042

[205] There are exceptions. One unusually aware group of sociologists recently warned their colleagues in the profession: 'Any assessment of how social origin impacts education, and of how education impacts social outcomes will be severely biased' if it continues to ignore the 'heritability in ability.' Martin Diewald, Tina Baier, Wiebke Schulz and Reinhard Schuck, 'Status attainment and social mobility' *Kölner Zeitscrift für Soziologie und Sozialpsychologie*, vol.67, 2015, p.378. Interestingly, though, none of the authors is employed in a British university, and their article was published in a German academic journal.

merit variables.[206] In its place, he and his co-author Richard Breen adopt an approach in which only the meritocracy hypothesis is subjected to empirical test (and is then found wanting).

The way they do this is to measure how much class of origin/class of destination odds ratios change when ability and motivation are added into their models.

They focus on social mobility between the extremes of the occupational class system – between Class I (higher-grade professionals, administrators, and officials, plus managers of large industrial establishments and large proprietors) and Class VII (semi- and unskilled manual workers and farm labourers). Their initial odds ratio comparing Class I and Class VII origins and destinations is 20.7 for males and 16.3 for females. When merit variables (ability test results at age 11 and the motivation score at 16) are added, they report that these ratios fall to 11.1 for men (a drop of 46 per cent), and to 6.3 for women (a drop of 61 per cent). If a single measure of qualifications is also then added, these ratios fall still further, although they do not report the final figures (from their data I calculate them to be just 7.4 for men and 3.3 for women – representing additional falls of 33 and 48 per cent respectively).

Goldthorpe and Breen claim these results disprove the meritocracy hypothesis because 'inequality is far from eliminated when "merit" variables are brought into the analysis.'[207] But this is a sleight of hand. Their approach

---

[206] He refers to this approach as a 'variable race' and refuses to engage with it, even though modelling like this is standard procedure across the social sciences. It is ironic that, having opposed this sort of approach in my work, he later adopted it himself when he started looking at influences on educational attainment (see the discussion of Truth #10, above)

[207] 'Class inequality and meritocracy', op cit., p.17.

starts out with a relatively small correlation (the association between class of origin and class of destination) and shows that it isn't entirely eradicated when we take into account a much bigger correlation (the association between IQ and class of destination). They then conclude from this that the small correlation is as, or more, important as the big correlation! This is clearly fallacious reasoning. As Gary Marks notes, 'Their conclusion of strong effects for class of origin and weak effects of ability are due to the methodological approach.' Had they started out cross-tabulating class of destination with ability, and then added class of origin, they would have found the latter had little impact.[208]

Class origins do have *some* effect on class destinations. Nobody ever claimed occupational placement was *completely* driven by ability and hard work. But in Goldthorpe's approach, class of origin is assumed to be the principal driver, and IQ is required to mop up the entire effect in order to refute it. Anything left unexplained by the merit variables is attributed to SAD factors. Right from the outset, the model is biased.[209]

---

[208] Gary Marks, *Education, social background and cognitive ability*, op cit., p.98.

[209] Much of the unexplained co-variation that remains after 'merit' has been taken into account will be due to (a) measurement error in the three control variables (the ability test score at age 11, the answers to ten motivation questions at age 16, and a measure of the overall level of qualifications people have achieved), plus (b) the effect of other variables that have not been included in the model (including other aspects of individuals' personalities) which vary with parental class. In his later work on educational attainment, Goldthorpe himself acknowledges that other personality factors like 'self-control' and 'self-efficacy' may be important in explaining the association between parents' class and children's achieved destinations – Bourne et al, 'Persistence of the social', op cit., p.20

Truth #17

A working class background is not a significant disadvantage in getting a middle class job, but a middle class background may help avoid a lower class job

When earlier (Table 1) I compared Goldthorpe's 1972 survey findings with what we would have expected to find had both the fathers and sons in his study been recruited to social classes purely on the basis of their ability, we saw that there was one mobility path which did not fit the perfect meritocracy model, and that was downward mobility from middle class origins to a working class destination. There was 'too little' downward mobility.

This suggests that class advantages may be playing a role in protecting some less intelligent middle class children from falling into the working class. This is confirmed by analysis of the 1958 birth cohort study where we saw that some relatively low-ability middle class children still managed to retain a middle class position as adults, and that private schooling, parental support and high parental aspirations all contributed something to the occupational status they achieved by age 33. It seems reasonable to conclude that factors like these are the main impediments to our achieving a perfect meritocracy.

This is consistent with a 2015 Social Mobility Commission report based on an analysis of the 1970 birth cohort. The author, Abigail McKnight, traces what happened by age 42 to children from higher income/higher social class families who scored poorly on a range of simple cognitive tests they did at age 5.[210] She finds they ended up in better jobs (in terms of class and income) than their early cognitive scores suggest they 'should' have done if the recruitment system were purely meritocratic. Using a series of regression models, she flags four key factors as important in explaining how they did it: their parents' level of education, their maths scores at age 10, the type of secondary schools they attended (state grammar and independent schools both helped), and their attainment of a university degree.[211]

She speculates that highly-educated parents helped less able middle class children over-achieve by, for example, helping them with their homework and exam preparation, guiding them towards the best schools, and mobilising their social connections to find them good jobs, although she offers no evidence to support these suppositions. As for the advantage gained by attending a grammar or independent school, she accepts this might reflect genuine value-added (i.e. these schools get more out of their pupils than other schools do), but she suspects employers of favouring private school applicants because of their accents and demeanour (but again offers no evidence).

McKnight advocates 'removing barriers that block downward mobility.'[212] However, it is one thing to devise

---

[210] Abigail McKnight, *Downward mobility, opportunity hoarding and the "glass floor"* Social Mobility Commission, June 2015, p.39

[211] Two of these four factors (the maths test score at 10 and the university degree) are, of course, themselves measures of their achievement (rather than of their more advantageous upbringing). What McKnight is basically claiming is that these people got better scores in maths at age 10, and later earned a university degree, even though their test results at five suggest they weren't bright enough. She puts this down to their parents' education (particularly if their parents were graduates) and to their schooling.

[212] *Downward mobility, opportunity hoarding and the "glass floor"*, op cit., p.42. Other than outlawing unpaid internships, most of the policies McKnight recommends actually have more to do with helping bright working class children succeed than removing privileges from less able middle class ones.

policies aimed at helping working class children succeed, but quite another for the government deliberately to set out to force more middle class children to fail. This is unlikely to find favour with many middle class voters (and they now make up getting on for half the electorate).[213] More importantly, it also seems perverse to demand that the government use its powers to counter the positive effects of strong and supportive parenting – something ministers say they want to encourage among all parents.

Devoting government time and resources to increasing middle class downward mobility also looks like taking a huge and controversial sledgehammer to crack a very small nut. It is almost certainly true that having pushy parents and attending a good school does help some less able middle class children to 'over-achieve' to some extent (although there are grounds for suspecting that McKnight's research may exaggerate the extent of this 'problem').[214] Downward mobility from the middle class does seem to be a bit stickier than it 'should' be if the system were perfectly meritocratic, but (as we shall now see), this does not look like a major policy priority.[215]

---

[213] Having said that, we shall see later that the government's Office for Students is now forcing more middle class children to fail by pushing universities to demand higher entry requirements from middle class applicants.

[214] It is possible that McKnight's findings partly reflect the failure of cognitive tests at age 5 to record accurate measures of these children's true ability. The fact that those who went on to successful careers scored so much better in a maths test at age 10 than in the simple cognition tests at age 5 suggests an element of regression to the mean, similar to that which severely weakened Feinstein's work, discussed earlier. She herself accepts this is a possibility, although she believes she has minimised it by combining reading, vocabulary, copying and drawing skills into a standardised single measure at age 5. My analysis of the 1958 birth cohort found a strong association between reading and numeracy test scores at 7 and cognitive test scores at 11.

[215] In their recent book, Bukodi and Goldthorpe also agree that the effect of social origins on class destinations operates mainly through preventing downward mobility rather than hindering upward mobility: in their words, it 'contributes more to the creation of glass floors than glass ceilings' (*Social mobility and education in Britain*, p.157).

Truth #18

**Middle class children enjoy more financial support, they
learn 'soft skills', and their parents can network –
but none of this makes a lot of difference to the
class people end up in**

John Goldthorpe suggests that middle class parents manage
to protect their less able children from downward mobility
by mobilising what he calls 'the regime's important *self-maintaining* properties.'[216]

What are these self-maintaining mechanisms? He
identifies two main types: (a) 'defensive expenditure' by
middle class parents aimed at preserving their children's
'competitive edge' over working class children (e.g.
buying private schooling, paying for extra tutoring, buying
houses in favourable school catchment areas, and helping
pay off student debt), and (b) the fostering of 'soft skills'
(things like middle class manners, or a middle class accent)
and advantageous social networks. These are the social
advantages and disadvantages which he believes explain
how a (roughly) 3:1 advantage in favour of middle class
children has largely been sustained over a period of 75
years, despite all the attempts by governments to erode it
through educational reforms.

This focus on 'defensive expenditure' plus 'soft skills and
networks' is the default explanation of much of today's social

---

[216] Goldthorpe, 'Understanding – and misunderstanding – social mobility in
Britain', op cit., p.443

mobility literature. A 2017 report by the Boston Consulting Group for the Sutton Trust, for example, identifies defensive expenditure as the principal means by which the middle class prevents its children from sliding downwards: 'A key barrier to mobility in higher education is wealthier parents' ability to build a "glass floor" by spending greater resources on their children's education.'[217] The report gives as evidence of this 'barrier': expenditure by 'wealthier families' on extra-curricula activities and private tuition; families moving house to get into a favoured state school's catchment area; and greater access to information and networks relevant to getting into Oxbridge. It also claims that children from 'wealthier backgrounds' benefit from greater parental support and parental networking, and know the 'soft skills' necessary for succeeding in 'an increasingly competitive job market.'

There is nothing new in any of this – sociologists have been writing about this sort of stuff since at least the 1960s. We've known for more than fifty years that middle class children are more likely to enjoy a bedroom of their own where they can do their homework; their parents are more likely to attend meetings at their school; they often get a head-start in reading because their parents read to them from an early age; they learn to speak a more formal 'elaborated' linguistic code which helps them at school with abstract reasoning; they may benefit from private tuition or even go to fee-paying schools; they are more likely to be encouraged by their parents to go to university or to aim for a high-status job; their parents may have useful contacts who can be mobilised to help ease them into jobs; and so on. All of this has been copiously well documented.

---

[217] Boston Consulting Group and Sutton Trust, *The state of social mobility in the UK,* July 2017, p.15. Note the linguistic sleight of hand, incidentally: an inventory of middle class 'advantages' becomes a 'barrier' against working class access.

The question, though, is how much difference does it all make?

We have already seen that 'defensive expenditures', like investment in private schooling, can make a small difference. Independent schools seem to squeeze better exam results out of children of equivalent abilities, and they turn out more confident and aspirational youngsters. In this way, they give less intelligent middle class offspring a better chance of clinging on to middle class membership.

Soft skills and networks may help a bit too. Friedman and Laurison looked at people who have achieved jobs in the top social class (higher-level managerial and professional occupations). They found that some had received financial help from their families that enabled them to go for a top job in the first place (e.g. the 'bank of Mum and Dad' helped them to live in London, where the best-paid jobs are). Some benefited from their parents' social networks (e.g. requesting advice from professional friends of their parents to prepare for interviews). And some enjoyed cultural advantages which helped them 'fit in' to their new jobs more easily (having been raised in middle class homes, they knew 'the rules of the game', felt more confident about putting in for a promotion or demanding a pay rise, and were more assertive in meetings). High-fliers from working class backgrounds, by contrast, reported feeling less certain and more anxious in their new positions. Friedman and Laurison say that these people sometimes 'eliminated themselves from pushing forward in their careers,' settling for middle-ranking professional positions rather than pushing on to the very top.[218]

---

[218] Freedman and Laurison, *The Class Ceiling*, op cit., location 3631.

It is easy to see how the various factors identified in this research (financial support from parents, patronage by superiors, useful contacts, 'fitting in') may have some effect on career development. But the fact remains, when we try to measure *how much* impact they have, these advantages appear quite marginal, and certainly not enough to account for a disparity ratio between the achievements of middle and working class youngsters as high as 3:1, which is commonly reported in social mobility research.

The proof of this can be found in the path model based on the 1958 birth cohort and summarised in Figure 3. That model shows no *direct* effect from class background to class destination at age 33. It contains no measures of 'soft skills' or 'parental networks,' but if these unmeasured factors had been playing a significant part in influencing people's social class destinations, this would have shown up as a direct effect from their parents' class to their own destination at age 33. The fact that there was no such direct effect tells us that these missing factors could not have been having a significant impact, once everything else was taken into account.

To the extent that class background influenced where people ended up in this path model, it was entirely mediated through its association with factors which were included in the model (things like motivation, aspiration, private schooling, etc.). This leaves no explanatory place for additional class advantages like 'contacts' or 'accents.' This is not to deny that such advantages may have a marginal significance in some instances for some people – but when we look at causal factors operating across this whole sample of several thousand people, they simply did not register. Everything that is statistically important about social background is already in the model.

Goldthorpe's talk of 'self-maintaining properties' reproducing class advantages is not, therefore, very convincing.[219] Indeed, in his latest book (with Erzsebet Bukodi) he comes close to admitting this himself.

Reviewing evidence from the 1970 birth cohort, Goldthorpe reports that 'the most surprising finding' is that help from parents when finding a job was 'of no great importance' in influencing which social class people ended up in. He notes there is 'very little evidence' to support the idea that parental and family networks help middle class youngsters avoid downward mobility into working class jobs. And he concludes that, 'Direct parental help is not a "non-meritocratic" factor of any great importance in determining the degree of individuals' success in working life within the population at large.'[220]

This is not to deny that social advantages like attending a private school do help some middle class youngsters over-achieve – rates of downward mobility from the middle class are not as high as they 'should' be in a perfect meritocracy, and merit variables do not mop up all the explained variance in our regression and path models predicting occupational

---

[219] Gary Marks comes to the same conclusion via a different route. He asks, if 'privileged families' have been able to outmanoeuvre educational reforms for the last 75 years in order to 'maintain their relative advantage', then why haven't they used this power to extend their advantage over the working class, rather than just maintaining it? (Marks, *Education, social background and cognitive ability*, op cit., p.172). Particularly over the last 20 or 30 years, as income and wealth inequalities have widened, why haven't middle class parents extended their children's lead over working class children by upping their 'defensive expenditures', for example?

[220] *Social mobility and education in Britain*, pp.163, 164-5 and 167. He ruefully concludes that, whatever the precise advantages are that middle class parents are able to provide for their children to help them get middle class jobs, his analysis has failed to identify them: 'We have therefore to recognise that DESO [the direct effect of social origins] is likely to result from a wide variety of social processes and to involve a range of other factors than those that we have been able to identify' (p.165).

status at age 33. But directing so much attention to issues like money, soft skills and networking while ignoring or downplaying ability and motivation is failing to see the wood for the trees. To the extent that middle-class origins help you get a good job, it is mainly because they contribute to cognitive ability and to ambition, motivation and hard work – not because of your accent, or who you know.

Truth #19

Top professions recruit more from the middle class than the working class, but this does not mean they are biased against working class applicants

The highest social class in the system of Socio-Economic Classification used by the Office of National Statistics consists of people working in 'higher managerial, administrative and professional occupations.'[221] Friedman and Laurison's analysis of the social origins of these top people (based on data from the Labour Force Surveys between 2013 and 2016) shows that half of them started life in middle class families. Only 10 per cent of working class youngsters get this far.[222] Children from the middle class are 6.5 times more likely than working class children to get one of these top professional jobs.

This study found that people in the top *professions* are more middle class in origin than those occupying senior *management* positions (in either the public or private sectors), and that the tops of the *traditional professions* like law, medicine, architecture and journalism are more middle class in origin than the tops of the *technical professions* like engineering or IT. Professional engineers, for example, are twice as likely to have originated in the middle class than in the working class,

---

[221] Office of National Statistics www.ons.gov.uk/methodology/
classificationsandstandards/otherclassifications/
thenationalstatisticssocioeconomicclassificationnssecrebasedonsoc2010
[222] Sam Friedman and Daniel Laurison, *The Class Ceiling*, op cit.

but architects are seven times more likely to have come from the middle class, and doctors are twelve times more likely. What's more, the children of lawyers and doctors are much more likely to go into these professions than other children: the sons and daughters of lawyers are 17 times more likely than other people to become lawyers, and doctors' children are 24 times more likely to become doctors.[223]

Is this because the professions are putting up barriers against working class entry? Or is it that youngsters born .into professional homes are more likely to be drawn to these occupations, and that many from working class backgrounds choose not to apply?

In 2009, the Social Mobility Commission admitted it was more the latter than the former. It identified various aspects of the selection and recruitment process into the professions which might be deterring working class applications – things like the use of unpaid internships to gain work experience, and the tendency of employers to recruit from a relatively small number of top universities rather than encouraging applications through more unconventional routes.[224] But it also recognised that the gulf in aspirations between children from different class backgrounds was a major factor. While 56 per cent of children of professional parents aspired to a professional career, this was true of only 13 per cent of children with parents in the lowest social class (semi- or unskilled occupations). Parental expectations, it concluded, were 'the key,' for many working class children either do

---

[223] Sam Friedman and Daniel Laurison, *The Class Ceiling*, op cit.

[224] It found that professional people generally grow up in more affluent families than the rest of the population, and that doctors and lawyers in particular come from markedly better-off backgrounds (their parents earned sixty per cent more than the average family income). Half or more of barristers, solicitors, doctors, journalists and chief executives attended independent schools when they were growing up *Unleashing Aspiration* op cit.

not think about going into a professional career, or do not want one.

The report made 88 recommendations for how to expand opportunities for working class youngsters to enter professional careers – extending professional outreach and mentoring, focusing on teaching young people the 'soft skills' which many professions require, increasing use of 'contextual' admissions into universities (i.e. taking account of candidates' social background), paying interns, and so on. The assumption seemed to be that if you lead working class kids to the professional water trough, they will start drinking.[225]

The 2009 report was clear that the 'problem' was not that the professions were deliberately putting barriers in the way of working class applicants – it was that good working class candidates were not applying in sufficient numbers and were sometimes going unrecognised. Quotas, it said, would do little to change this, and it explicitly ruled out positive discrimination in favour of working class applicants on the grounds that targets or quotas would undermine the principle of appointment on merit, and would therefore create unfairness.[226]

---

[225] It is striking in so much of this literature how researchers and politicians (themselves members of the professional class) assume that, given the opportunity, everyone would 'obviously' opt for a professional career, just as they did. There are all sorts of rational reasons why working class youngsters (or middle class youngsters, for that matter) might prefer to follow other career paths, but this issue of preferences is rarely unpacked. As Robert Plomin notes in *Blueprint*, you can give people opportunities, but you can't force them to take them: 'Genetic differences in aptitudes and appetites influence the extent to which children take advantage of opportunities. To a large extent opportunities are taken, not given' (op cit., p.96).

[226] 'Some have suggested that the way to achieve this is through various forms of positive discrimination to reverse the inequalities in access to professional careers. We reject this. We believe it would not work, and instead could create new kinds of unfairness. Our aim should be to improve the overall quality of intake to the professions by widening the pool of qualified candidates, rather than by introducing new forms of discrimination that could undermine the principle of admission by merit' – *Unleashing Aspiration*, op cit., p.45

Three years later, however, the Commission's tone had changed. In a follow-up report, it was much sharper in its criticism of the professions themselves. It attacked leading employers for focusing their graduate recruitment on a small number of 'socially exclusive' top universities where working class youngsters were under-represented.[227] It criticised employers for demanding evidence of prior relevant work experience (which working class candidates are less likely to have). And it complained that professions put too much emphasis on formal qualifications (where middle class applicants tend to out-perform working class ones). In his introduction to the report, Alan Milburn claimed the professions were 'closing their doors instead of opening them,' and he accused the senior ranks of the professions of running 'a closed shop.'[228]

Three years after that, in 2015, the Commission published a qualitative study of recruitment practices in top law and accountancy firms which reinforced many of these criticisms. Noting that entry into these firms was 'heavily dominated at every entry level by people from more privileged socio-economic backgrounds,'[229] this report pinned the blame clearly on firms' recruitment practices (targeting a small band of 'elite' universities) and on their screening procedures (selecting candidates for shortlists based on their academic qualifications and their performance in cognitive tests). It urged employers to cast their nets wider than Oxbridge and

---

[227] 'The overwhelming evidence suggests that too many professional employers still recruit from too small a cohort of universities. Since those universities are the most socially exclusive in the country, these recruitment practices merely reinforce the social exclusivity of the professions' Social Mobility Commission, *Fair Access to Professional Careers: A progress report* 2012, p.24

[228] *Fair Access to Professional Careers: A progress report* 2012, op cit., p.4

[229] Louise Ashlery, Jo Duberley, Hilary Sommerlad and Dora Scholarios, *A qualitative evaluation of non-educational barriers to the elite professions* Social Mobility Commission, June 2015, p.6

the Russell Group universities, to abandon screening based on academic credentials, and to play down evidence of past performance as a guide to people's suitability for posts.

By 2015, therefore, the Social Mobility Commission was seriously suggesting that employers should stop recruiting so many people from the best universities, should ignore academic qualifications when drawing up interview shortlists, and should disregard people's prior achievements when making job offers.

This sharp shift away from the principles of meritocratic recruitment was justified on the grounds that talent is 'not an objective concept but rather rooted in a system of values which are permeated by assumptions about class.'[230] We have encountered this claim before. It is the dogma popularised by the Marxist sociologist, Pierre Bourdieu. Translated from the Marxist jargon, it is saying that 'ability' is just an ideological smokescreen which enables employers to equate middle class behaviour and mannerisms with 'talent.' This then results in middle class recruits getting privileged access to jobs and promotion within the professions, even though they are no more talented than their less successful working class competitors.

What evidence is there that this actually happens? The authors of the 2015 report refer us to the work of Sam Friedman and Daniel Laurison who in turn rely heavily on Bourdieu. Bourdieu suggests that 'sets of dispositions' like accent, posture, manners, vocabulary and cultural tastes are used in class societies as signs of superiority. In their research among top professionals in a TV company, an accountancy firm, an architecture practice and the acting profession, Friedman and Laurison apply this idea to

---

[230] *A qualitative evaluation of non-educational barriers to the elite professions*, op cit., p.26

explain why those recruited from middle class backgrounds are more likely to get to the very top positions. They claim, for example, that senior staff identify 'people like themselves' as potential high-fliers to take under their wing, and that middle class entrants who already understand the culture of the firm show more confidence and become more assertive in meetings. 'It is,' they say, 'the privileged who are most comfortable adopting, mastering and playing with dominant behavioural codes.'[231]

There is probably something in this. If you grow up the son or daughter of an academic, you will feel a lot more familiar with the ways of the universities, and if your father is a QC you won't feel out of a place entering one of the Inns of Court. Equally, if you grow up the son or daughter of a professional footballer you are more likely to feel at home on the training ground of a professional football club, and if your dad was a bus driver you probably feel comfortable hanging around in bus depots. Parents everywhere pass on experience and wisdom (what the academics call social and cultural capital) to their children, bequeathing different kinds of advantages whenever the opportunity allows.[232] None of us enters the world of work on completely equal terms.

The real question, though, is whether any of this means that talented and motivated people from other backgrounds are being shut out of top professional jobs.

Friedman and Laurison admit they 'observed very limited evidence of what might be called overt discrimination' in the professional settings they studied.[233] Nobody was

---

[231] *The Class Ceiling*, op cit., location 682

[232] 'The UK is certainly not unique. In nearly all high income countries it is possible to discern a similar link between origins and destinations' *The Class Ceiling*, op cit., location 751

[233] *The Class Ceiling*, op cit., location 4787

deliberately selecting less talented middle class candidates ahead of more talented working class ones. Notwithstanding Milburn's rhetoric, the professions were not 'shutting their doors' to working class applicants, and they did not 'shut up shop' so as to exclude people from other social backgrounds than their own. Even the use of unpaid internships seems to have less effect in excluding bright working class candidates from the professions than has often been assumed.[234]

It makes sense for the professions to encourage more youngsters to apply with outreach schemes and mentoring, and quite a few firms (many of them legal and financial services companies) are nowadays doing just that.[235] But to tell selection panels that they are wrong to pick the best-qualified applicants for interview, or that they should not go to the highest-ranked universities to find them, is absurd. Why would an employer disregard paper qualifications when they provide such a strong guide to people's talents and aptitudes? Given the fierce competition to get into Oxbridge, why wouldn't employers go there to find the best graduates? Telling employers to reduce their recruitment from the most selective universities, or to ignore people's qualifications when drawing up their interview shortlists, looks like the antithesis of meritocracy, not its fulfilment.

---

[234] Analysing the 1970 birth cohort data, Bukodi and Goldthorpe suggest that concern over unpaid internships has been 'somewhat exaggerated,' although they accept that there may be certain professions where such internships do provide middle class youngsters with a significant leg-up (*Social mobility and education in Britain,*p.167).

[235] Some have even set their own social mobility targets. The Social Mobility Foundation is a charity, based in the City of London, which aims to widen career opportunities for disadvantaged sixth-formers, and it publishes an annual 'Social Mobility Employer Index' which scores companies on seven criteria assessing their efforts to attract, retain and promote lower class applicants. KPMG came top in 2018. See government Press release, *Top 50 UK employers for social mobility* 21 June 2017, www.gov.uk/government/news/top-50-uk-employers-for-social-mobility

Truth #20

Many of the top positions in our society are occupied by people who went to Oxford or Cambridge – but this does not make Britain 'deeply elitist'

According to a 2014 Social Mobility Commission report, 75% of judges, 59% of cabinet ministers, 57% of permanent secretaries, 47% of newspaper columnists, 33% of BBC executives, 18% of FTSE 350 chief executives, 14% of vice-chancellors, 12% of the names on the *Sunday Times* rich list and 6% of chief constables and police & crime commissioners went to either Oxford or Cambridge University.[236] Should we be worried about statistics like these?

The answer depends on how youngsters get into Oxford and Cambridge in the first place. Given that these are our two top universities (Oxford currently ranks fifth in the whole world with Cambridge sixth),[237] it should not come as a surprise to learn that quite a few of the four thousand British 'leaders' in different fields of endeavour identified by the Commission studied there. Indeed, it might be considered strange if substantial numbers of people filling the country's top positions in public administration, business, politics and the law had *not* been educated at one of our top universities.

But that's not the way the Commission sees it. Its report

---

[236] Social Mobility Commission, *Elitist Britain?*, op cit., pp.14-15

[237] 2019 QS rankings https://www.topuniversities.com/university-rankings/world-university-rankings/2019. Imperial (8th), University College London (10th) and Edinburgh (18th) are the only other UK universities to make the top twenty.

poses the (supposedly rhetorical) question of whether 'the sheer scale of the dominance of certain backgrounds' means that top jobs are 'more about who you know than what you know.' It wonders if the dominance of Oxbridge means 'some talent [is] being locked out?'[238] And in his introduction to the report, Alan Milburn leaves us in no doubt that 'a dramatic over-representation of those...educated at Oxbridge' is 'locking out a diversity of talents.' Not for the first time, Milburn complains of what he calls a 'closed shop at the top.' Britain, he concludes, 'is deeply elitist.'[239]

Charges like these might make sense if Oxford and Cambridge recruited unfairly. But we have seen that they do not. Both universities insist entrants achieve high A-level grades, and once the quality of A-levels is factored in, neither of them shows any bias towards private school applicants or candidates from middle class homes. These are scrupulously meritocratic institutions, which is precisely what the Social Mobility Commission is supposed to be in favour of. So why wouldn't employers go fishing for top talent there?

To complain that the top positions in our country contain too many Oxbridge graduates makes no more sense than attacking the manager of the England football team for selecting most of his players from the top Premier League clubs. Where else would you expect to find the most talented players?

---

[238] *Elitist Britain?* op cit.
[239] *Elitist Britain?*, op cit., p.2

Truth #21

Cognitive ability is not the only personality trait that varies between social classes and contributes to social mobility

In Michael Young's formulation, meritocracy rewards 'ability plus effort.' Thus far we have focused mainly on the importance of cognitive ability in shaping educational and occupational outcomes. But what more can we say about the importance of effort?

Effort is more difficult to define than ability and is certainly more difficult to measure, for there is no single, summary statistic corresponding to the general factor, g, in IQ tests. 'Effort' is likely to involve all sorts of personal qualities including perseverance, self-control, determination, ambition, self-confidence, honesty, reliability, originality, independence, a willingness to learn ('openness'), sociability and much else, and these sorts of qualities are rarely measured in studies of social mobility.

Earlier (Truth #15), we equated 'effort' with 'motivation' at school as measured by indicators like absenteeism, teacher ratings and students' answers to attitude questions about schoolwork. Even this rough-and-ready measure revealed that 'effort' has a significant influence on educational and occupational outcomes. In the 1958 birth cohort, motivation at school ('ambition') at age 16 accounted for 15 per cent of the explained variance in the occupational status people had achieved by age 33. This made motivation the second most important explanatory factor after cognitive ability. It had twice the impact of parents' class.

There is, however, more to 'effort' than just motivation at school, and we need more sophisticated measures to analyse it. A US study of High School students found that, while motivation at school was an important influence on the level of income and occupational status they achieved later in adulthood, there were other personality traits which also played a significant role.[240] Motivation alone does not fully capture important aspects of personality that may be shaping people's class destinations.

We have known for a long time that personal character traits vary between different social classes. Michael Argyll noted in 1994 that 'social skills' (what today we call 'emotional intelligence', qualities like empathy, supportiveness and seeing another's point of view), are associated with social class (middle class children as young as 8 appear on average more 'socially competent' than their working class peers).[241] Working class people are also likely to be more impulsive, and are on average significantly more aggressive, while middle class children are on average more achievement-oriented, and have a stronger sense of their own ability to control the things that happen to them (what psychologists call 'locus of control).

Argyle noted that these qualities are often linked to upward mobility. Among men who get promoted into managerial positions, for example, 'achievement motivation' and what he called a 'need for power' (a desire

---

[240] Marion Spengler, Rodica Damian and Brent Roberts, 'How you behave in school predicts life success above and beyond family background, broad traits and cognitive ability' *Journal of Personality and Social Psychology*, vol.114, 2018, 620-36.

[241] Michael Argyle, *The psychology of social class* op cit., chapter 7.

for influence and responsibility without worrying unduly about being popular) are important attributes. Energy, vitality and self-discipline (i.e. responding rationally to problems without getting angry) are also all associated with upward mobility.

More recently, in an analysis of the 1958 UK birth cohort, Michelle Jackson found clear links between personality traits and social mobility patterns. Children who exhibited signs of withdrawal, anxiety and inhibition at age 11 (as reported by teachers) were significantly less likely to end up in professional/managerial jobs by age 42 (regardless of their cognitive ability, educational qualifications and class of origin).[242] Personality also influences the type of middle class position upwardly mobile people move into. Movement into managerial positions tends to be associated with low withdrawal/anxiety scores at age 11 (suggesting that employers aim to recruit confident, outgoing people into these jobs), whereas movement into higher-level technical jobs tends to be associated with low aggression scores at age 11 (presumably because these careers reward patience and passivity). Professional recruitment showed no bias either way.

Like IQ testing, personality measurement is time-consuming, so complete personality profiles are rare in longitudinal surveys of social mobility. The 1970 UK birth cohort did, however, include direct psychological tests, conducted at age 10, which were designed to measure children's self-esteem and 'locus of control.' It also included (less rigorous) assessments by their teachers of

---

[242] Michelle Jackson, 'Personality traits and occupational attainment' *European Sociological Review*, vol.22, 2006, 187-99. This is a rare example of a sociological study of social mobility which takes both cognitive ability and personality seriously.

the children's level of anti-social behaviour, relations with peers, attentiveness and extraversion.[243]

All these scores correlated significantly with the social class of the children's parents, and most also predicted the level of qualifications they went on to achieve as adults (even after controlling for their class background). Attentiveness in particular had a markedly strong effect on educational attainment. Boys deemed to be anti-social at age 10 were significantly more likely to be unemployed as adults (they tended to get jobs but then lose them), while those who scored highly on extraversion were the least likely to experience joblessness. As regards incomes in adulthood, boys with high self-esteem, and girls with high locus of control and/or strong behavioural scores (e.g. good peer relations), all tended to earn more (even controlling for their class of origin).

Leon Feinstein, who reports these findings, concludes that behavioural and psychological factors may explain a large chunk of the association between class of origin and class of destination: 'Although it is far from being the case that these scores explain all the variance in outcomes that would otherwise be proxied by social class differences, they have been shown to do so to a significant extent.'[244] So personality types vary across the classes, and this helps explain why children from different class backgrounds achieve different educational and occupational outcomes.

Another analysis of the 1970 birth cohort, conducted when participants reached age 30, confirms that class-related personality traits measured in childhood exerted

---

[243] See Leon Feinstein, 'The relative economic importance of academic, psychological and behavioural attitudes developed in childhood' *Centre for Economic Performance Paper*, no.443, 2000.

[244] Feinstein, 'The relative economic importance of academic, psychological and behavioural attitudes developed in childhood' op cit., p.22

an independent influence on the income and occupational status attained later in life by panel members.[245] This analysis suggests that behavioural attributes and high intelligence often reinforce each other, for bright children tended to become more confident (they developed a higher 'locus of control') and they behaved better in the classroom. This combined effect of IQ and character then influenced their later careers. This is consistent with my own finding from the 1958 birth cohort that motivation and ability reinforce each other.

The Millennium birth cohort (born in 2000) has also been studied in an attempt to analyse the links between 'character capabilities' and class backgrounds.[246] Noting that 'application', 'self-regulation' and 'empathy' all help predict educational and occupational success later in life, Lexmond and Reeves looked at five year-olds and found that all these traits varied according to their social class backgrounds. Middle class children are more likely to exhibit the personality traits that help people succeed in life.

---

[245] Sophie von Stumm, Catherine Gale, G David Batty, Ian Deary, 'Childhood intelligence, locus of control and behaviour disturbance as determinants of intergenerational mobility' *Intelligence* vol.37, 2009, 329-40

[246] Jen Lexmond and Richard Reeves, *Building Character* London, Demos, 2009

Truth #22

Like cognitive ability, 'effort' is to a large extent genetic

The big question remains: why do these crucial personality traits tend to vary among children from different social class backgrounds? Lexmond and Reeves think the reason lies in socialisation, and in particular, different styles of parenting. Children whose parents link affection with a structured environment – what the report called 'tough love' – tend to develop positive traits most strongly, and they often come from middle class homes (so-called 'tiger parenting' is an extreme example of this).[247] Children whose parents are 'disengaged' develop them least successfully, and they are often found in working class homes.

There is, however, a different and more compelling explanation for why personality traits in young children vary by the social class of their parents. Robert Plomin provides evidence that every dimension of personality is strongly heritable (i.e. personality is to a large extent transmitted from parents to children through their DNA). He insists that parenting per se has little effect on the development of personality characteristics.

The reason 'disengaged' parents may appear to raise children lacking in qualities like 'application', 'self-regulation' or 'empathy' is not because of their parenting styles; it is because their genes make these parents

---

[247] Amy Chua, *Battle hymn of the tiger mother* Penguin 2011

disorganised, uncaring or over-aggressive, and the same genes show up in their children where they get expressed in anti-social behaviour, poor attention spans, and so on. Plomin is quite explicit about this: 'Parents don't make much of a difference in their children's outcomes beyond the genes they provide at conception.'[248]

If this is right, then early childhood interventions intended to compensate for the effects of poor parenting are unlikely to have much of an impact on social mobility patterns in the future. Personality is being inherited through the genes, not taught through early socialisation. As Plomin warns: 'The environmental levers for change are not within our grasp.'[249]

Psychologists traditionally identify five core dimensions of personality: openness to new experiences, conscientiousness and self-discipline, extraversion (including assertiveness and sociability), agreeableness (cooperation and trustworthiness) and neuroticism (anxiety and mental stability). All five vary by social class. Lower class occupations tend to be associated with higher scores on neuroticism and agreeableness, and with lower scores on conscientiousness, extraversion and openness.[250]

A 2007 review of six different longitudinal studies in America found that extraversion, neuroticism, conscientiousness and agreeableness measured in adolescence all

---

[248] Plomin, *Blueprint*, op cit., p.83.

[249] Plomin, op cit., p.101. Gregory Clark (*The Son Also Rises*, Princeton University Press 2014) makes a similar point in his review of studies comparing adopted and natural children. These show that 'most of the variation in outcomes for adopted children stems from their biological parents or from chance, not from their adoptive parents' (p.264). Furthermore, 'It is not clear that public policies can do much to change family environments in the ways that matter to the social outcomes for children' (p.268).

[250] B. Chapman, K. Fiscella, I Kawachi and P. Duberstein, 'Personality, Socioeconomic Status, and All-Cause Mortality in the United States' *American Journal of Epidemiology*, vol. 171, 2010, pp. 83-92

helped predict occupational status 46 years later, even after controlling for social class origins. Indeed, the impact of these four personality variables on social class destinations was, according to the authors, comparable with that of IQ and class origins. These authors also reported a clear link between weak self-control and high aggression in childhood, and the risk of unemployment in adulthood.[251]

Similar results have been reported in the UK. Several hundred people in Aberdeen who completed IQ tests in 1947, when they were aged 11, were contacted again more than half a century later, at age 64, and were given personality tests.[252] The researchers found that class origin, IQ and education had all directly affected the socio-economic status these individuals had achieved in adulthood, but so too had their level of neuroticism (the higher they scored on neuroticism, the lower their occupational status was likely to be). Low neuroticism is associated with a high 'locus of control' (the belief that you can control your own destiny), and the authors speculate that this may explain why it is linked to social mobility. They also found that openness had an indirect effect on occupational attainment as a result of its influence on educational attainment. Openness, they say, is linked to creativity, and creative people tend to perform better in education.[253]

---

[251] Brent Roberts et al.,'The power of personality' *Perspectives on Psychological Science*, vol.2, 2007, 313-45. The authors suggest that personality may affect occupational outcomes in various ways: people select the jobs which best suit their character, employers choose certain types of people for certain types of positions, people leave jobs for which they are not suited, they try to mould their jobs to fit in with their personalities, and individuals with certain personality traits are simply better at doing certain kinds of tasks.

[252] R. Staff, M. Hogan, L. Whalley, 'The relative economic importance of academic, psychological and behavioural attitudes developed in childhood' *Personality and Individual Differences*, vol.114, 2017, 206-12

[253] Although they did not find any significant association between class of destination and the other three main personality traits (extraversion,

The 1958 birth cohort did not include measures of the 'Big Five' personality characteristics, but as in the Aberdeen study, participants did complete personality tests much later (in this case, when they were aged 50). Education and childhood IQ scores remained the strongest predictors of changes in occupational status between 33 and 50, but personality variables (in particular conscientiousness and openness) also had 'modest but significant effects' on people's social mobility trajectories. These two personality variables also correlated to some extent with cognitive ability scores recorded at age 11, again confirming that a high IQ and high levels of motivation reinforce each other.[254]

Michael Argyle noted more than twenty years ago that aggressiveness is 50 per cent heritable and is significantly related to low attainment later in life. More recently, Robert Plomin reports that extraversion and neuroticism are both 40 per cent heritable. As we have seen, he suggests there is no aspect of personality that is not strongly shaped by our DNA. This is now being confirmed by the results of gene-wide association studies; research has found more than one hundred SNP associations for neuroticism, for example.[255] The heritability of personality traits, and their association with social class, suggests that (like IQ), these characteristics may play a significant part in explaining why children born to middle class parents tend on average

---

conscientiousness and agreeableness), the authors note that other, 'more powerful' analyses have reported direct effects for these too ('The relative economic importance of academic, psychological and behavioural attitudes developed in childhood' op cit., p.210).

[254] Helen Cheng and Adrian Furnham, 'Childhood cognitive ability, education and personality traits predict attainment in adult occupational prestige over 17 years' *Journal of Vocational Behavior* vol.81, 2012, 218-26

[255] Plomin, *Blueprint*, op cit., p.130

to achieve better educational and occupational outcomes than those born to working class parents, but a lot of research still remains to be done in this area.

Truth #23

Most social mobility studies ignore households where nobody has a job or is earning an income, yet these are likely to include the most disadvantaged people

Research on class mobility has generally been limited to individuals who have jobs, for class mobility is defined by movement between different occupational positions. Similarly, studies of income mobility tend to be limited to individuals who live off earnings, ignoring those who live solely on benefits. The consequence is that long-term welfare recipients who are marginal to the labour market, and whose income is made up entirely of state benefits, have often been excluded from both the sociologists' and the economists' social mobility models.[256]

This is a huge and astonishing gap in the social mobility literature which rarely gets mentioned or acknowledged. It means we know very little about the mobility chances of children growing up in what may be the most disadvantaged homes, yet these are the very individuals who might be expected to suffer the greatest problems as they grow older.

---

[256] Sociologists do sometimes include those without jobs by allocating them to their partner's social class (based on his/her occupation) or to their most recent social class (based on the last occupation in which they were employed). But many disadvantaged people will still be excluded even under these rules, and those that are included will get mixed in with an occupational class, rather than analysed separately, and in this way disappear from view. As for economists' studies of income mobility, those without earnings get dropped, which is one reason why the Sutton Trust's work on the 1958 and 1970 cohorts ends up using less than 20 per cent of the sample.

What little we do know about this group often comes, not from studies of social mobility, but from research on poverty (the fact – noted at the start of this report – that 80 per cent of children born to parents under the poverty line are no longer in poverty when they reach adulthood is, for example, the product of research on poverty by the Joseph Rowntree Foundation). But not all jobless people are poor, and not all poor people are jobless – these are not synonymous categories – so we cannot substitute the mobility experiences of the poor for those of the long-term jobless.

Recently, however, some social mobility reports have begun to include people who are not active in the labour market. Researchers studying pupil attainment in schools often lack information about parents' occupations and incomes, so instead they have had to adopt as their indicator of social disadvantage a household's eligibility to claim free school meals (FSMs). Households claiming FSMs generally have a high level of dependency on welfare, and low or zero activity in the labour market. Fortuitously, therefore, this neglected but crucial group of marginal households has at last started to figure in social mobility research.

Unfortunately, there has been a tendency in these studies to equate these long-term jobless households (many of which are single-parent families) with the 'working class' identified in more conventional social mobility research. In reality, these are two very different social strata. In 2018, 13.7 per cent of primary and 12.4 per cent of secondary school pupils received free school meals. This is a relatively small, welfare dependent group (about one-eighth of all families with children). By contrast, 24 per cent of people covered by the Labour Force Survey were defined as 'working class.'

Most people employed in relatively low-skilled work do not qualify for FSMs.[257]

When it comes to their educational performance, children receiving free school meals generally do much worse than other children (even those from 'routine' working class homes). The 2019 *State of the Nation* report finds that in Year 1 at school, only 70 per cent of FSM children reach the expected standard in decoding phonics, compared with 84 per cent of other children. By age 11 (key stage 2), only 46 per cent have reached the expected standard in reading, writing and maths, compared with 68 per cent of other pupils; at age 16, only 40 per cent get grade C or better in GCSE English and maths, compared with 68 per cent; and by age 19, just 16 per cent of them achieve 2 A-level passes, compared with 39 per cent.[258]

How much of this difference in attainment is down to intelligence and effort, and how much is due to social disadvantage? The answer is: we don't know, because as usual, this research contains no evidence on the cognitive ability levels of these children.

The assumption of the researchers is that the differences in children's attainment levels are down to the social

---

[257] The Social Mobility Commission is guilty of confusing these two distinct strata in its 2019 *State of the Nation* report where it treats FSM claimants and people in working class jobs as interchangeable categories. The report begins with data from the Labour Force Survey, which (obviously) only includes people in paid work, comparing those in low-skilled working class jobs with those in professional-managerial class occupations. But then in later sections it switches to comparing 'the most disadvantaged' children with 'the most advantaged' ones. By 'most disadvantaged,' it means children whose parents are claiming FSMs, and 'the most advantaged' are everyone else. The report never makes clear, however, that 'the working class' children discussed in its opening chapter and 'the most disadvantaged' children discussed in later chapters are two very different groups.

[258] Social Mobility Commission, *State of the Nation 2018-19* op cit., pages 27-39. In addition, 26% are in HE at age 19 compared with 43% non-FSM (p.87), and 5% get to top-third HE institutions compared with 12% (p.88).

disadvantages suffered by their parents (in particular, the low level of welfare benefits they receive). But given everything we have learned about social class and achievement, it would be surprising if intelligence (and other genetically-driven personality traits like agreeableness and conscientiousness) was not also a strong factor in explaining their educational shortfall.

Having said that, research has repeatedly documented the negative impact on child development and wellbeing of social factors like unmarried teenage motherhood,[259] the absence of a committed father, the lack of an employed adult role model, lack of parental engagement with children, lack of parental interest in their education,[260] and a general absence of domestic structure and rules. Many of these risk factors are highest among welfare-dependent, long-term jobless households claiming free school meals.

In 2018, 43 per cent of FSM kids failed to reach a 'good' level of development by the time they started school at age 5, compared with 26 per cent of non-FSM children.[261] A 'good' level of development is defined by 17 criteria identified in the government's Early Years Foundation Stage *Profile Assessment Framework*.[262] They include: how

---

[259] The Sutton Trust recognises that being born to an unmarried teenage mother is one of the strongest predictors of poor school performance and low earnings in all western countries. Teenage motherhood in the UK is about twice as common as in other Anglophone countries such as Australia and Canada. Lee Elliot Major and Stephen Machin, *Social Mobility and its enemies*, op cit., p.30

[260] My research with Rod Bond on the 1958 national birth cohort found that parental interest and involvement in their children's education raises the chances of their children's educational and occupational success, but that it is linked to the ability of the child. Parents tend to get more involved and interested if their children are bright and do well at school – there is a positive feedback loop – and this in turn encourages the children themselves to raise their aspirations. In the case of less able children, however, parental interest and support tends to tail off quite early.

[261] Social Mobility Commission, *State of the Nation 2018-19* op cit., p.23

[262] https://assets.publishing.service.gov.uk/government/uploads/system/uploads/attachment_data/file/790580/EYFSP_Handbook_2019.pdf

well a child pays attention when spoken to; whether it can follow instructions; can express itself verbally; coordinate its physical movements (e.g. use a pencil); get dressed and use a toilet independently; show confidence in dealing with new situations; work in a group; show sensitivity to the feelings of others; read and write simple sentences; count and perform simple addition and subtraction; understand measures of size, weight, distance, time and money; know about differences within their own community and the wider world; recognise the uses of technology; sing songs, dance and use their imagination.

Some of this, we know, will reflect innate differences, a function of the DNA bequeathed by parents to their children. But specific, simple skills like the ability to use a toilet, count from 1 to 10, or coordinate physical movements should not be beyond the capacity of any but the most disabled of school-age children. The fact that some five year-olds struggle with them says a lot about the cultural environment in which they have spent their early years. In particular, the big gap in these skills between FSM and non-FSM children almost certainly reflects cultural deprivation and/or neglectful parenting as much as any innate differences in ability or personality.

Why should social factors play an important part in children's developmental scores at the bottom end of our society when we have seen from recent research in behavioural genetics that parenting makes little difference on average to how children turn out?

The explanation is that behavioural geneticists calculate their statistical probabilities across the whole population. Most parents do a good job of bringing up their children, so there is little overall variation. If we focus down, however, on the smaller number of cases towards the more extreme end of the distribution where poor parenting may be more concentrated, the impact of parenting variations on child development starts to show up more clearly. As Plomin explains: 'Genetic research describes the normal range of variation, genetically or environmentally. Its results do not apply outside this normal range... Severe environmental problems such as neglect or abuse can have devastating effects on children's cognitive and emotional development.'[263] What applies to the bulk of the population does not therefore necessarily apply as we approach the tail.

---

[263] Plomin, *Blueprint*, op cit., p.85

Truth #24

Britain does not have a serious 'social mobility problem', but it may have a serious 'underclass problem'

On average, long-term jobless parents produce less well-adjusted children who behave poorly at school, achieve fewer qualifications, and are more at risk of unemployment when they reach adulthood.

According to the 2019 *State of the Nation* report, the likelihood of an eleven year-old child from a non-working household engaging in bullying, disobedience or anti-social activity is 1½ times greater than that of a child from the bottom rung of the working class, and is almost 6 times greater than that of a child from a professional/managerial background. Children from non-working (basically FSM) households are twice as likely as those from routine working class homes to exhibit emotional symptoms like nervousness, lack of confidence and intense worrying, and are almost three times as likely to do so as the children of professional parents.[264]

A similar pattern emerges for truancy and exclusions from school. Fixed period exclusions from school (i.e. suspension short of expulsion) run at around 10 per cent

---

[264] It's the same story with hyperactivity, which was a bit more common among children from non-professional homes back in 1969, but where the class gap has increased significantly since then. By 2012, the risk ratio between higher professionals' and routine workers' children had swollen to 2.3, and it was even higher in the case of the FSM children.

for those eligible for free school meals, which is twice the rate of other students. Truancy (which is linked to lower educational attainment) is around 16 per cent for the FSM group, 11 per cent for others.

All of these behavioural problems are known to increase the risk of unemployment in adulthood. People who grow up in homes where there is no adult working are much more likely than other people to be jobless themselves when they reach adulthood.[265] The authors of a Nuffield College review for the Social Mobility Commission note that, 'Childhood behavioural problems are strongly associated with chances for social mobility, being linked to unemployment, lower incomes and wages, and lower educational attainment.'[266] This is confirmed by an analysis of the 1970 birth cohort which finds that behavioural problems identified at age 10 had a significant adverse effect on income and occupational status by age 42. These problems were more often associated with children from low socio-economic status families.[267]

The problems kick in early. In 2012, the then Education Secretary Michael Gove suggested that some children are 'actively harmed' by growing up in 'chaotic homes' where they are not 'effectively socialised,' and he gave examples of children starting primary school at age 5 who are still wearing nappies and who cannot tell the difference between a letter and a number. 'There are,' he said, 'significant numbers of children who, because of their home environment, arrive at

---

[265] Those in jobless households at 14 spend an extra 17 per centage points of their time out of work themselves. Sam Friedman, Daniel Laurison, Lindsey MacMillan, *Social mobility, the class pay gap and intergenerational worklessness* Social Mobility Commission, 2017, p.25

[266] L. Richards, E. Garratt and A. Heath, T*he childhood origins of social mobility,* Social Mobility Commission, 2016, p.50

[267] Abigail McKnight, *Downward mobility, opportunity hoarding and the "glass floor"* Social Mobility Commission, June 2015, p.25

school simply incapable of learning... They will grow up in circumstances so chaotic that it's not just a case that they are neglected, it is the case that they are actively harmed by the failure to be in a nurturing environment where their brain can develop.'[268]

When a Conservative politician from an earlier generation, Keith Joseph, said something similar to this back in 1974 (albeit in more robust language) he got so badly burned that his future political career was effectively trashed.[269] But although Gove's reference to an 'educational underclass' clearly rankled with some on the left, most people nowadays recognise the problems he was referring to are real.[270]

The Sutton Trust, for example, has identified 'troubled pupils' who suffer 'multiple dimensions of disadvantage' and 'years of instability, abuse and violence at home as young children.' Drawing on school case studies, the Trust's Chief Executive says of these youngsters: 'If they do attend school, they are unable to control their emotions, with frequent outbursts of anger. They are prone to impulsive behaviour and low moods, and have few friends. Often they are moved from one school to the next. They are at risk of

---

[268] Tim Ross, 'State must aid pupils from chaotic homes, says Gove' *Daily Telegraph* 24 October 2012

[269] His speech, in October 1974, identified a 'culture of poverty' which was holding back some children from the poorest backgrounds. The section of the speech which caused the most controversy was when he said: 'A high and rising proportion of children are being born to mothers least fitted to bring children into the world ... Some are of low intelligence, most of low educational attainment. They are unlikely to be able to give children the stable emotional background, the consistent combination of love and firmness ... They are producing problem children.' Joseph was forced to withdraw from the Conservative Party leadership election, where he was challenging Edward Heath, and according to Wikipedia, he repeatedly apologised for his comments, but to no avail.

[270] Lee Elliot Major and Stephen Machin, *Social Mobility and its enemies*, op cit., p.125

[271] *Social Mobility and its enemies*, op cit., p.125

drug addiction and involvement in gangs.'[271]

It was an American political scientist, Charles Murray, who first brought the plight of children like this to public attention in Britain thirty-odd years ago by claiming that a British 'underclass' was emerging characterised by low average intelligence, a high rate of single parenthood, high levels of involvement in criminality and substance abuse, and a history of welfare dependency.[272] In a pioneering attempt to test some of these claims, Alan Buckingham used the 1958 birth cohort data to identify a small group (just over 5 per cent) of men and women who, by the age of 33, had exhibited weak attachment to the labour market and a high level of dependency on state welfare payments, including social housing. He compared this 'underclass' stratum with unskilled workers at the lowest rung of the working class and found several significant differences in their life histories.

As Murray had predicted, Buckingham found the underclass group scored significantly lower on average on cognitive ability tests at age 11 than even the unskilled workers, and they were much more likely to have left school at 16 with no qualifications. As early as age 11 they were more likely to have been diagnosed as 'hostile, aggressive, restless and anxious' or 'withdrawn, depressive and inhibited'. By age 16, they were 50 per cent more likely to have been in trouble with the police and twice as likely to have been accused of a crime. Quizzed on a range of attitudes at age 23, underclass men were much less committed to a work ethic than were men in the unskilled working class. They

---

[272] Charles Murray, *The emerging British underclass*, Institute of Economic Affairs, 1990. There was a series of follow-ups including *Underclass: The crisis deepens* (IEA 1994), *Charles Murray and the underclass* (IEA with The Sunday Times, 1996, and *Underclass +10* (Civitas with the Sunday Times, 2001).

were also much less likely to have married (or even had a steady partner) by age 33. Meanwhile, underclass women were much more likely to have become single mothers.[273]

This is not primarily a matter of low income, for youngsters growing up in working class homes may be little better off economically than those raised in workless households. It is more likely to have something to do with parenting and family neglect. According to the 2019 Social Mobility Commission report, parenting may be more important in the early years than socio-economic factors: 'The range and quality of activities which parents undertake with pre-school children is more strongly associated with children's social and intellectual development as compared with either parental education or occupation.'[274]

So why is parenting sometimes so bad? It could be that people with particular traits, generated by their genes, behave in chaotic, aggressive, short-term, uncontrolled ways, and these genes are passed on to their kids who do likewise. Those lucky enough to inherit better DNA escape the vicious cycle (and despite all the problems, there is mobility upwards as the poverty data prove). As Plomin says, environmental influences in childhood are not insuperable, for there are plenty of examples of individuals raised in appalling circumstances who nevertheless come good as adults.

Clearly, though, a chaotic home where children are parked in front of a television all day and nobody bothers

---

[273] Average ability scores (out of 80): underclass 33, class VII 38. No qualifications: underclass 45%, class VII 28%. Strongly agree that would pack in a job they didn't like, even if no other job to go to: underclass 39%, class VII 16%. Unmarried males at 33: underclass half, class VII one-fifth. Single mother at 33: underclass half; class VII one-eighth. Alan Buckingham, 'Is there an underclass in Britain?' *British Journal of Sociology*, vol.50, 1999, 49-75.

[274] Social Mobility Commission, *State of the Nation 2018-19* op cit., p 30

even to make sure they get up and go to school must make life a whole lot harder, even for those born with the ability and personality traits needed to achieve success. How can such circumstances be changed? The 2019 Social Mobility Commission report sets a lot of store by the extension of free, early years childcare, for this at least gets children out of their wretched home circumstances for a while and exposes them to more enriching experiences.[275]

Public spending on early years education has increased from under £1 billion in 1997-8 to around £5.4 billion in 2015-16 and is expected to hit £6 billion by 2020.[276] Today, all three and four year-olds are entitled to fifteen free hours of pre-school per week (soon to rise to thirty), and the poorest kids can get places from the age of two. Nevertheless, the Social Mobility Commission reports that all this expenditure seems to have had little impact so far on the mobility chances of children from FSM homes.[277]

---

[275] Social Mobility Commission, *State of the Nation 2018-19* op cit., p.29

[276] Social Mobility Commission, *Time For Change: An Assessment of Government Policies on Social Mobility 1997-2017* London, June 2017

[277] *Time for a change*, op cit.

PART THREE
SOCIAL MOBILITY MADNESS

The never-ending pursuit of meritocracy

There are clear differences in the average educational and occupational achievements of children born into different classes. These differences have proved fairly persistent over a long period of time. But they are not due to unfair 'blockages' placed in the way of those trying to come up from below, even though many commentators think they must be. We have seen that universities are scrupulously meritocratic in their selection procedures, for example, and that employers in the professions and elsewhere are generally committed to appointing the best candidates, irrespective of their social origins.

Neither are these differential outcomes due mainly to unfair 'privileges' enjoyed by the children of the middle classes, even though a huge amount of research effort has been devoted over the years to working out what these privileges might be, and how they might be removed.

Social advantages and disadvantages do play a small part in shaping people's lives. We have seen how middle class children in independent schools are more likely to realise their full potential than working class kids attending the local 'bog standard' comprehensive. We have also seen that many parents seek to give their children a head start in life by encouraging them, reading to them, making sure they are fully prepared to start school, and that middle class homes may be better equipped on average to do this than some working class homes.

It is also true that some children seem to enjoy an 'inside track' when it comes to careers. We have seen how the children of doctors, for example, are more likely to enter the medical profession themselves. Parents are role models (for good or ill), and doctors can provide their children with better practical help, support and guidance in getting to medical school than other parents can. Meanwhile, at the opposite end of the social spectrum, we have also seen how some children grow up in neglectful or abusive homes where they never see an adult get up and go to work, where parental affection is in short supply, and where criminality and substance abuse are commonplace. It is difficult to see how young lives could fail to be blighted by circumstances such as these.

Given all this, nobody could claim that Britain is a perfect meritocracy. But no country is. Just because the system is not perfectly meritocratic does not mean it is not broadly meritocratic. Nor can it easily be made more meritocratic. Quite the reverse, in fact, for the more open we become, the harder it is likely to be to squeeze the last bit of meritocracy out of the tube.

For all the concern that gets expressed about private schools, elite universities, exclusive professions, pushy parents, social networks and the rest, we have seen that it is people's natural ability, in combination with other genetically-governed personality factors affecting their drive, tenacity and motivation, that are the principal factors determining where they end up in the class structure of modern Britain. Ability and motivation are by far the key drivers of success in our society – and these are the two elements that together underpin a meritocracy.

It is therefore perverse that so few researchers pay them any serious attention. Cognitive ability has routinely been overlooked in analyses of social mobility, and many researchers – even today – refuse to include it in their work. There is almost a wilful refusal to see the evidence. A flawed study appearing to show that class overwhelms natural ability in children's early development is still being used by influential researchers to discredit the idea that innate ability matters, even though it is known to be false and misleading.

When it comes to analysing intelligence, there is a lot of bad faith around. Even researchers who reluctantly agree to include measures of cognitive ability in their analysis set up their statistical models in such a way as to minimise its effects. Yet developments in our understanding of genetics conclusively demonstrate that differences of intelligence (and most other personality attributes) are grounded in our genes and are profoundly important in shaping the different educational and class destinations we arrive at. Social mobility research which fails to measure these differences is likely to be badly biased and grossly misleading in its findings – and today, that's most of it.

Social mobility researchers have been selling policy-makers short by ignoring cognitive ability. But politicians do not seem particularly unhappy about this, for they too are reluctant to take on board the importance of innate differences of intelligence. It is much easier politically to tell your voters that the system is rotten and that you know how to fix it, than to acknowledge that the system is remarkably open and the reason their child has failed to secure a top job is because he or she simply isn't bright enough, or didn't work hard enough.

Determined to iron out differential outcomes which they think have been caused by social advantages and disadvantages, each generation of politicians sets out to eradicate the barriers. The result has been several decades of fervent reform. But all this effort has achieved disappointingly small effects. It has often been costly, disruptive and hugely destructive, but the class differences stubbornly persist.

Back in 1944, it was fairly obvious that there was a class bias in access to the education system. The move to a completely 'free' system of state secondary education, where all children competed in a single, national examination for places at grammar and technical schools, was intended to fix it. But children from middle class homes continued to out-compete children from working class homes in the new 11-Plus examination. Working class children were getting into grammar schools in much greater numbers than before the war, but the pass rate was still skewed. Academics and political activists concluded that the reform had failed.[278]

---

[278] There is little doubt that the 11+ was a blunt instrument for sorting out intellectual sheep and goats. Some bright working class children failed when they 'should' have succeeded, while some dull middle class children passed when they 'should' have failed. But the system did not misclassify substantial proportions of children. A. H. Halsey, a colleague of Goldthorpe's on the original social mobility project, analysed the educational backgrounds and experiences of Goldthorpe's sample of ten thousand men and showed that those born into middle class families had been over-represented in selective (state and private) secondary schools (A. Halsey, A. Heath, J. Ridge, *Origins and Destinations: Family, Class and Education in Modern Britain* (op cit.). However, he then estimated average IQ scores for individuals from different social class backgrounds on the basis of data collected in the 1950s (when sociologists still believed that such scores meant something and were worth collecting). This produced average IQ estimates of 109 for those originating in the professional-managerial class, 102 for those from intermediate class backgrounds, and 98 for those born to working class parents. Working with these estimates, Halsey calculated the proportion of children from each class who 'should' have attended a selective school had the system been perfectly meritocratic. While 72% of professional-managerial class sons attended selective schools, Halsey's calculations suggested that only 58% were bright enough to have done so. And while 24% of working class sons attended such schools, the calculations indicated that 28% should have done so given their IQ. This suggests a 24% middle class over-representation in grammar schools, and a 17% working

Thus began a long search for the cause of the class bias, and a solution to put it right.

Some thought the problem was in the home. Middle class parents were gaining an unfair advantage by paying for their kids to be coached for the 11-plus exam. Or middle class children enjoyed an unfair advantage because their parents had books at home, read to them at bedtime, gave them their own room where they could study, attended parents' evenings at the school, and transmitted higher aspirations to their offspring.[279]

Others suspected the problem was in the schools. Middle class teachers were subconsciously discriminating against working class pupils by using forms of language (an 'elaborated linguistic code') unfamiliar to kids from lower class environments who were therefore struggling to keep up. The curriculum itself, some said, reflected middle class experiences, and working class children found it difficult to relate to it (the grammar schools in particular felt 'alien' to many working class children). And there was a strong consensus that the 11-Plus exam was 'culture bound' and that its IQ test in particular was skewed in favour of middle class candidates.[280]

Drastic measures were called for.

When Labour won the 1964 General Election, Harold Wilson appointed Charles Anthony Raven Crosland as his

---

class under-representation. One in four middle class grammar school pupils should not have been there, and one in six working class pupils at secondary modern schools should. Nevertheless, Halsey's results also show that cognitive ability was by far the most important single factor distinguishing those who succeeded under the old 11+ system and those who failed.

[279] For example, Jack Douglas, *The Home and the School* MacGibbon & Key 1964

[280] See, for example, Basil Bernstein, 'Social class and linguistic development' in A. Halsey et al (eds), *Education, economy and society* Free Press, 1961; Brian Jackson and Dennis Marsden, *Education and the working class* Routledge 1962; A. Halsey, A Health and J. Ridge, *Origins and Destinations* op cit.

Minister for Education. The son of a senior Civil Servant and product of one of Britain's most prestigious independent schools (Sir Roger Chomeley's School at Highgate in London), Crosland was an Oxford don who hated the state grammar schools. When Wilson made him Minister for Education, Crosland went home and told his wife: 'If it's the last thing I do, I'm going to destroy every fucking grammar school in England.'[281]

In 1965, Crosland issued an instruction to all local education authorities to close down their grammar schools and replace them with 'comprehensives' which would be forbidden to select pupils by ability. Only a few local councils resisted. Within a few years, Crosland had succeeded in wiping out all but 163 of nearly 1,300 grammar schools in England and Wales (another 179 'Direct Grant' schools continued to syphon off some of the brightest children until they too were scrapped in the 1970s).[282] It was the biggest act of state vandalism in England since Henry VIII demolished the monasteries.

By scrapping selection at eleven, and teaching all children together in the same schools, the new 'comprehensive system' was intended to eradicate the middle class advantages that the tripartite system had inadvertently reproduced. But very rapidly, the familiar pattern reappeared. Middle class children clustered in disproportionate numbers in the higher streams of the comprehensive schools, and they continued to out-perform working class children in post-16 examinations and university entry.[283]

---

[281] Susan Crosland, *Tony Crosland*, Jonathon Cape 1982

[282] Figures from House of Commons Library, *Grammar School Statistics*, March 2017. Direct Grant schools were independent grammars, outside the state system, which received government grants in return for offering some free places to children selected in the 11-Plus exam. When this system was scrapped, most of them went fully independent.

[283] Julienne Ford, *Social class and the comprehensive school* Routledge 1969

The obvious response to this, much favoured in the 1970s, was to weaken or abolish streaming.[284] If mixed ability schools weren't working, try mixed ability classrooms. Testing was pared back, classroom rankings were abolished to weaken competition, classroom seating plans were changed to encourage group learning, reading schemes were revised, teaching of formal grammar was all but abandoned (too 'middle class'), rote learning of tables and poetry was scrapped, and more 'progressive' methods of teaching were introduced. But despite all this upheaval, working class kids continued to 'under-perform' relative to those from middle class backgrounds.

Perhaps the problem lay with the quality of the teachers? Teaching was made an all-graduate profession in an attempt to 'raise standards in the classroom,' and training colleges and universities made sure their trainees learned all about social class biases in education and how to overcome them.

Or maybe the intake into comprehensive schools wasn't sufficiently mixed? Middle class parents often avoided the worst-performing comprehensive schools by buying houses close to the better ones, so local authorities began to redraw their catchment area boundaries to trap them. More recently, some have abandoned the principle of parental choice altogether, allocating school places by ballot to force social class mixing.

It was noted that many working class kids were still leaving school at the first opportunity, before getting any formal qualifications, so in 1972 the minimum leaving age was raised to 16 to force them to stay longer, as many middle class pupils already did.[285] In 1960, only 12 per cent

---

[284] Brian Jackson, *Streaming: An education system in miniature* Routledge 1964
[285] On early leaving and the anti-school subculture among working class boys, see Paul Willis, *Learning to Labour* Saxon House 1977

of pupils remained at school beyond the age of 15; forty years later, 70 per cent were staying beyond the age of 16.[286] But that still didn't make much difference to attainment gaps, so the Blair government legislated in 2008 to force everyone to stay in education or training up until the age of 18 so that nobody would finish their education without some sort of qualification. Yet still the social class imbalance in educational achievement persists.

Educationalists began to suspect that the problem was rooted in the very early years of children's development, before they ever started school. Children raised in poor families were, they suggested, receiving less intellectual stimulus in these crucial early years than middle class children did, and this was impairing their cognitive development.

The Major and Blair governments responded with free child care and nursery school places for the under-fives (a policy which also won favour with women's rights campaigners by enabling more mothers to return to work before their children started school). A national network of Sure Start centres was set up, aimed mainly at poorer children, although (predictably) middle class parents soon started taking advantage of them as well. But as we saw earlier, the Social Mobility Commission says all this effort has had precious little impact on the mobility chances of the poorest children.[287]

Radical changes have also been introduced at the other end of the education system. The university sector was expanded in the sixties, when eight new 'plate glass' universities were founded, and then almost doubled in size in 1992 when the former Polytechnics were transformed into universities. When he came to power, Tony Blair set a target

---

[286] Gary Marks, *Education, social background and cognitive ability,* op cit., p.167.
[287] Social Mobility Commission, *Time for a change* op cit.

for half of all young people aged 18 to 30 to go into higher education, and in 2017 his aspiration was all but fulfilled when the figure reached 49 per cent.[288]

But there was no point in herding half the population into higher education if you don't give them a piece of paper at the end of it, so nearly everyone who completes a university course has to be allowed to graduate. This is difficult to engineer when academic ability is normally distributed in the population (relatively small numbers at the high and low extremes and most of us near the middle). With universities recruiting further and further down the ability distribution curve, a radical expansion of student numbers should have resulted in a big reduction in the proportion of good degrees and an expansion in the number of poor degrees and fails. What actually happened, however, was the exact reverse.

In 1995, when 291,000 students were given places at UK universities, just 7 per cent of graduates achieved first class degrees and another 40 per cent got upper seconds. By 2018, after student numbers had almost doubled to 533,000, the number of firsts had mushroomed to 28 per cent and upper-seconds had increased to 51 per cent. The explanation is grade inflation. Work that would have been awarded an upper (or even lower) second in the past today gets a first. This situation has become so farcical that the government recently threatened universities with fines if they continue to expand the number of first class degrees they award.[289]

---

[288] Richard Adams, 'Almost half of all young people in England go on to higher education' *The Guardian*, 28 September 2017. 27 per cent of 18 year-olds go to university straight from school. According to the Social Mobility Commission, there were 200,000 students in Britain in the 1960s. Today there are 2.6 million (*A qualitative evaluation of non-educational barriers to the elite professions*, 2015, p.23).

[289] Sources: Paul Bolton, 'Higher Education Student Numbers' (House of Commons Library *Briefing Paper* 7857, February 2019); Higher Education Statistics Agency web site (www.hesa.ac.uk/data-and-analysis/students/outcomes); Gemma Tombs and David Hughes, *Analysis of degree classifications over time* (Office for Students, 2018); Camilla Turner 'Universities who continue to give out too many top grades face £500,000 fines, Education Secretary warns' *Daily Telegraph*, 24 March 2019

Grade inflation also hit the schools. How else could half a million youngsters every year get good enough A-level grades to be admitted to university?[290] Up until the late 1980s, no more than 10 per cent of A-level candidates achieved A grades, but then the numbers started increasing. In 1990 they reached 12 per cent; in 1997 (when Blair came to power) they had grown to 16 per cent; and after that, they ballooned, reaching an extraordinary 27 per cent by 2010 (when a new A* grade had to be introduced to differentiate the excellent candidates from the rest).

It was much the same story with the 16-plus school examinations. Through the sixties, seventies and eighties, the proportion of 16 year-olds gaining five O-levels or CSE grade 1 passes (regarded as equivalent) remained fairly constant at between 20 and 25 per cent. But then the two exams were spliced together in 1988 to stop 'bias' against working class pupils, many of whom used to follow the less taxing CSE syllabus rather than the more academically-challenging O-levels. Following the launch of the new GCSEs, the pass rate started climbing. In 1988, the first year of the new GCSEs, the number of candidates achieving five or more passes at grades 1-3 (the old O-level equivalent) reached 30 per cent. By 1997 it was up at 45 per cent. It finally topped out at a whopping 82 per cent in 2013 before Education Secretary Michael Gove intervened to stop the madness.[291]

---

[290] Data on A-level and o-level/GCSE results from Joint Council for Qualifications website, www.jcq.org.uk/examination-results/

[291] For a long time, politicians and educationalists insisted the staggering rise in the pass rates of GCSE, A-level and degree examinations was due to improved teaching and greater student diligence. In reality, it had much more to do with a softening of the syllabus and an easing of assessment standards (often made possible by a shift away from traditional examinations to include more coursework and teacher assessments).

Employers soon got wise to the dilution of educational standards. With nearly half of all youngsters coming out of universities clutching degrees, more demanding employers started recruiting only from the top universities. So now politicians are doing something about this too, moving to ensure that more lower class kids get into the top universities even if they don't have the necessary A-level grades.

As we have seen, the Social Mobility Commission has attacked the top universities for being 'elitist.' It wants them to make greater use of 'contextual admissions' – an innocuous-sounding phrase which means making lower grade offers to lower class students.[292] The Office for Students (the higher education regulator) agrees with this. All universities seeking to charge fees above £6,000 per annum now have to agree an 'Access and Participation Plan' with the OfS, which for the top universities means increasing their intake from areas of the country which are officially defined as 'less advantaged.'

The OfS has given Russell Group universities twenty years to eliminate the admissions gap between richer and poorer students.[293] To achieve this, it suggests making offers as low as BBC (2 'B' grade passes and 1 'C' grade) to applicants from 'less advantaged' parts of the country (the standard offer at most top universities is AAB, and at Oxbridge it is

---

[292] *State of the Nation 2018-19,* op cit., p.98: 'Universities should be strongly encouraged to make more use of contextual admissions. This goes beyond simply making use of contextual data in their admissions process in the determination of whether to make an offer, but reducing the grade entry requirement depending on the background of the student.'

[293] Camilla Turner, 'Universities are making lower offers to poor students "under the radar" to avoid middle class backlash, report says' *Daily Telegraph,* 25 July 2019

at least AAA, and can be as high as 3 A*s).[294] Universities UK – which represents all 136 universities in this country – has gone along with this by affirming its commitment to 'tackling social mobility and inequality' with 'wider use of contextual admissions.'[295]

Responding to this pressure, Oxford recently agreed to offer places on lower grades to 50 candidates from 'severely disadvantaged' or 'educationally disrupted' backgrounds. Bristol is apparently accepting C grades from some applicants.[296] Both Oxford and Cambridge are reported to

---

[294]Jack Hardy, 'Oxbridge should consider poor pupils with one B and two Cs at A-Level for a place, universities regulator says' *Daily Telegraph*, 1 May 2019. Also Camilla Turner, 'Universities should introduce "privilege flags"' *Sunday Telegraph* 12 May 2019. The OfS denies that this would depress standards, suggesting that students admitted to Oxbridge with BCC grades at A-Level have an 80% chance of graduating with a degree and a 46% chance of getting a first or upper second. However, Oxbridge drop-out rates are very low (only 1.4% of Cambridge students fail to complete their degrees), and 94% of Oxford students get firsts or upper-seconds, so an 80% chance of graduating, and a 46% chance of getting a good degree, looks like a huge disparity (sources: https://www.tcs.cam. ac.uk/cambridge-university-has-uks-lowest-dropout-rate/ https://www.ox.ac.uk/ about/facts-and-figures/undergraduate-degree-classifications?wssl=1).

[295] Universities UK, *Working in Partnership: Enabling social mobility in higher education*, 2016, p.6. There has also been an extraordinary rise in the number of unconditional offers made to applicants by universities. In 2013, just three thousand people received unconditional offers. By 2018, this had grown to 68,000 (or to 117,000 overall, if we include all offers with some element of unconditionality) – *State of the Nation* 2018-19, pp.89 and 97. This astounding rise is partly the result of universities offering unconditional offers contingent on applicants agreeing not to go anywhere else (p.97) – a competitive strategy which the government is now trying to stop. But it is also due to universities responding to government pressure to increase their intake from lower class households. Twenty-eight per cent of these unconditional offers were made to youngsters applying from the most 'deprived' areas of the country (defined as the bottom quintile of the POLAR classification of neighbourhood disadvantage). The irony, noted by the Social Mobility Commission, is that applicants given unconditional offers tend to ease up on their studies and get worse A-levels than they would otherwise have done, so this trend is actually damaging lower-class students' attainment rates. Not for the first time, we find ourselves chasing our own tails.

[296] Gabriella Swerling and Camilla Turner, 'Oxford University agrees to let in disadvantaged students with lower grades' *Daily Telegraph*, 21 May 2019

have introduced a 30 per cent cap on admissions from private schools.[297] And Cambridge University's new 'access plan' for 2020-2025, submitted to the OfS in September 2019, proposes that applicants from private schools should in future be required to achieve higher A-level grades than those from state schools.[298] A previously meritocratic admissions system is being abandoned, step by miserable step.[299]

None of this is likely to satisfy the critics for very long, however. The Chief Executive of the Sutton Trust recently suggested that admission to our top universities should be determined by lottery. Set an academic baseline, she says, then select for Oxbridge randomly from among all those who score above this threshold. Unlucky losers could be given consolation prizes of places in lesser universities.[300]

Meanwhile, the Labour Party has set its sights on the independent schools. At the 2019 conference, the Party agreed to abolish charitable status for independent schools (ending their tax privileges), to cap university entrants from private schools at 7 per cent, and to seize their endowments,

---

[297] Sian Griffiths, 'Oxbridge "penalises" private pupils' *The Sunday Times*, 25 August 2019

[298] Sian Giffiths and Julie Henry, 'Private pupils may need higher grades to go to Cambridge' *The Sunday Times* 22 September 2019

[299] The OfS and the universities use a measure called POLAR ('Participation of Local Areas') to identify the least 'privileged' or 'advantaged' applicants. This divides all UK census wards into quintiles based on the proportion of 18 year-olds living there who participate in higher education. The universities themselves admit that this measure does not correlate strongly with other indicators of disadvantage (Universities UK, *Working in Partnership*, p.15), so deliberately skewing admissions offers in favour of applicants from 'disadvantaged' POLAR neighbourhoods is likely to introduce new sources of unfairness into what used to be a meritocratic system. As Lionel Shriver points out, many youngsters facing real adversity at home (e.g. alcoholism, domestic violence, bereavement, divorce, abuse, neglect) will not come from the so-called 'deprived neighbourhoods', so they will now be doubly disadvantaged by this policy ('Adversity is the new diversity', *The Spectator*, 25 May 2019).

[300] Major and Machin, *Social mobility and its enemies*, op cit., p.209-10

investments, land and buildings and transfer them into the state sector.[301] Fifty years after Labour abolished the grammar schools, it is now intent on finishing the job. In its determination to engineer equal outcomes, all children will in future be forced to attend the same state schools, and some of the oldest and finest educational institutions in the country will be closed as a result.

Reviewing this sorry half-century history of educational reform and upheaval, certain common patterns are revealed. Focusing solely on 'rectifying' unequal outcomes, with no serious regard for what might be driving them in the first place, successive government interventions have increased coercion (e.g. restricting school choice by parents, forcing kids to stay in education even if they don't want to, limiting the autonomy of universities to select their own students), dragged down standards (scrapping grammar schools and dumbing down GCSEs, A-levels and degrees), and undermined meritocratic systems of recruitment (e.g. forcing universities and employers to target applicants from certain kinds of backgrounds at the expense of others who may be better qualified). Yet all this zeal has achieved almost nothing in flattening social class differences in achievement (for middle class youngsters continue to do better on average than working class youngsters).

Yet the more resilient the apparent 'class bias' in outcomes proves to be in the face of each new initiative, the more the politicians ramp up the scale and ambition of their next intervention. Every reform is followed by an escalation of demands for more change. Rather than reflecting on why decades of social reform appear to have achieved so little,

---

[301] Richard Adams and Kate Proctor, 'Labour delegates vote for plan that would abolish private schools' *The Guardian online*, 22 September 2019

each generation of politicians blunders blindly on, stepping up the pressure for even more change, squandering even more public money, and trashing even more of our high-performing institutions – first the grammar schools, then A-levels, and now Oxbridge, the old professions and the independent schools. When it comes to chasing the social mobility chimera, nothing succeeds like failure.

Meritocracy or equality?

It would be wrong to say that nothing has changed over the long period since World War II. We have seen that social mobility rates have fluctuated over the years, with upward mobility expanding in the twentieth century with the growth in size of the middle class, and downward mobility increasing more recently as this expansion has slowed. Educational expansion, too, has meant that many more working class students now stay on at school, pass GCSE and A-level examinations, and get university degrees (although whether this has done them much good is another question).

But as Goldthorpe's work has demonstrated, the relative chances of people from different social class origins succeeding or failing in life have not shifted much over this period. Disparity ratios have tilted a little towards children from lower class backgrounds, but there has been no dramatic shift. Middle class kids are still two or three times more likely to get good jobs than working class kids. This is a persisting pattern which has led the Social Mobility Commission to express despair at what it calls 'our country's lamentable track record.'[302]

In 2017, the Commission published a report on the 'progress' made over the previous twenty years in creating

---

[302] Alan Milburn and Gillian Shephard, Foreword to *State of the Nation 2017*, op cit., p.iii

what it called 'higher social mobility' leading to a 'better, fairer and more inclusive' society.[303] The report examined policy reforms affecting the early (pre-school) years, the school years, post-school training/education, and employment, and in each case it awarded green, amber or red ratings according to the 'progress' that had been made in flattening out disparities in the achievement levels of people from different social class backgrounds. The results made for gloomy reading:[304]

- Early years policies got an amber rating: 'Given the billions invested in services, it is disappointing there has not been a greater impact on narrowing the attainment gap between poorer children and their better-off peers';

- Schooling policies also got an amber rating: 'Despite reforms to our schools and success in improving results and raising standards... the attainment gap between poorer children and their wealthier counterparts at 16 is as large as it was twenty years ago... This is totally unacceptable';

- Post-16 education and training fared worse with a red rating: 'The last two decades have seen major changes to post-16 education with the school age rising to 18, access to higher education being widened and apprenticeships being created. These reforms have consumed a significant amount of public money and government effort but progress has been too slow... Despite universities' success in opening their doors to more working class youngsters than ever before, retention rates and graduate outcomes for disadvantaged students have barely improved';

---

[303] Social Mobility Commission, *Time for a change* op cit., p.1
[304] *Time for a change* op cit, pages 3-4

- Employment policies, too, were rated red: 'Those holding top jobs have become slightly more socially diverse, although progress has been painfully slow.'

Overall, of 37 policies reviewed from the last twenty years, only 7 got a green light, and 16 were graded red. 'Public policy,' the report concluded, 'has not been as impactful as it should have been.' Why the lack of progress? The Commission was in no doubt. It was because governments have been insufficiently committed to promoting social mobility. Still more needs to be done.

It was Albert Einstein who is generally credited with the observation: 'The definition of insanity is doing the same thing over and over again, but expecting different results.' This captures what has been happening in successive governments' pursuit of increased social mobility in Britain. Driven on by the desire to reduce or even eliminate the difference between middle class and working class success rates, both in the education system and in the labour market, governments keep changing the rules, reforming the institutions and spending money, but very little change comes about as a result. If we do not wish to remain trapped indefinitely in this cycle of insanity, there are only two ways out.

One, favoured by the former head of the Social Mobility Commission as well as by the radical left in academia and politics, is to dismiss all the reform effort up to this point as mere 'tinkering' and get on with a root-and-branch, radical shake-up of our whole society.[305] What is needed, said Alan Milburn in 2017, is 'a more activist agenda... The old agenda has not delivered enough social progress. New approaches

---

[305] Government press release, 'Left behind Britain', 30 March 2017, www.gov.uk/government/news/left-behind-britain-narrowing-the-social-mobility-divide

are needed if Britain is to become a fairer and more equal country. It is time for a change.'[306]

John Goldthorpe, whose research has been central to sociological work on social mobility for more than fifty years, agrees with this. He thinks the focus on education has been a blind alley and that what's required is a full frontal attack on class privilege. He spelled out his view in an article in *The Guardian* in 2016: 'The period from the end of the Second World War to the present has been one of more or less continuous educational expansion and reform... Yet despite all this expansion and reform, inequalities in relative mobility chances have remained little altered... What can be achieved through educational policy alone is limited – far more so than politicians find it convenient to suppose. The basic source of inequality of educational opportunity lies in the inequality of condition – the inequality in resources of various kinds – that exists among families from different class backgrounds. And it is this inequality of condition that will have to be addressed.'[307]

In this view, if it's fairness you want, stop fiddling around with educational opportunity and focus on end-state inequalities instead. Raise taxes on higher earners, increase

---

[306] Alan Milburn, Foreword to *Time for a change* op cit., p.7. Shortly after writing this, he resigned as Chair of the Social Mobility Commission.

[307] John Goldthorpe, 'Decades of investment in education have not improved social mobility' *The Guardian* 13 March 2016. In his more recent work with Bukodi, while reiterating his belief that educational reform can do little to increase relative social mobility rates, Goldthorpe appears to distance himself from those (like Tony Atkinson) who believe the answer is more redistributive taxation and state intervention. His fear is that such policies are unlikely to gain widespread public acceptance, and he ends up suggesting there may be limits to what more can realistically be achieved to increase fluidity (*Social mobility and education in Britain*, p.220ff).

welfare benefits, expand the public services and take control of key parts of the economy.[308]

Not surprisingly, Jeremy Corbyn's Shadow Minister for the Cabinet Office – the Party's spokesperson on social mobility – finds this a very agreeable agenda. In 2017 he wrote in *The Guardian*: 'Low social mobility is associated with great inequality. The more a society consists of a rigid hierarchy of social class, the less meritocratic it is. Labour's goal, therefore, is surely to tackle inequality rather than the narrow pursuit of mobility… Might a radical government therefore convert the Social Mobility Commission into a Commission for Social Equality? I would hope so.'[309]

For the left, the old social-democratic agenda of equality of opportunity (Blair's 'education, education, education') has proved a dead-end. It is time to replace it with a more draconian socialist agenda emphasising equality of outcomes. This marks a return to Michael Young's position in the 1950s, for the very idea of meritocracy is now being jettisoned in favour of an egalitarian redistribution of rewards. To hell with 'just desserts.'

There is, however, a second possible route out of the recurring cycle of madness, and this is to recognise that what the politicians (and most of the public) say they want to achieve is, to a large extent, what we already have. We keep pursuing something we've already got. Far from rejecting

---

[308] There is, of course, nothing new in this argument. It was almost fifty years ago that Basil Bernstein published his famous essay entitled 'Education cannot compensate for society' (*New Society*, 1970, pp344–347).

[309] Jon Trickett, 'Social mobility isn't enough' *The Guardian* 1 December 2017. Note that Trickett's claim that low mobility is associated with greater inequality (based on the so-called 'Gatsby curve') has been discredited by the critique of cross-national mobility statistics reviewed earlier (John Jerrim, Alvaro Choi and Rosa Rodriguez, *Cross-national comparisons of intergenerational mobility: are the earnings measures used robust?* op cit.).

the idea of meritocracy, we should acknowledge it and start spreading the good news.

Britain is not a perfect meritocracy – no country is, or ever could be. Some people enjoy a better start in life than others, and a few are seriously disadvantaged by their upbringing. We have seen there are still changes we could make at the margins to even things up more. In particular, the plight of children born into households where nobody works, where parenting is neglected, and where criminality and substance abuse may be commonplace, is one that should concern all politicians, although this is not a social mobility problem so much as an underclass problem.

The solution for these children, if there is one, has nothing to do with shutting down Eton, organising lotteries for entry to Oxford, or stopping doctors' children from studying medicine. None of this will make the slightest bit of difference to the life chances of children at the bottom. Nor, for that matter, will redistributing income and wealth change much, for the source of their difficulty is not lack of money, but is chaotic behavioural norms and destructive cultural values and beliefs. Tackling these things takes us far outside the kinds of concerns which currently dominate the social mobility agenda and may call for some dramatically novel ideas.[310]

---

[310] Toby Young (the son of Michael Young) has suggested that one way of evening things up, once we can identify the DNA variations responsible for much of the difference of ability (and effort) between individuals, would be to allow low-income parents to screen embryos in vitro and choose the genetically most favoured one to bring to term. Young further suggests that richer parents could be prohibited by law from using this technology (see Toby Young, 'The fall of the meritocracy' *Quadrant*, 7 September 2015, and 'My own modest proposal: designer babies for the poor' *The Spectator*, 12 September 2015). Such a system of 'genetic redistribution' will certainly be possible before too long (Plomin thinks screening for personality characteristics will almost certainly happen), but Young's proposal encounters a number of objections. Would low IQ parents want to have a high IQ child who might grow up to make them look

Meanwhile, for the great majority of people, ability and hard work remain the principal drivers of success and failure in life. Social class origins play a much smaller role in shaping our destinies than many politicians believe, and many of the claims that are repeatedly made by politicians and commentators – that we live in an 'elitist' and 'closed shop' society, that talented people from the working class are 'blocked', that universities and employers are 'biased' when it comes to selecting people – are either completely untrue or hugely exaggerated. The evidence for this is easy enough to find. Most of the truths I have outlined in this report have been under our noses for a long time. It's just that politicians haven't been interested in looking at them.

This refusal to take on board the evidence has condemned us to an unending circle of social mobility initiatives which cost so much (in disruption as well as money) yet achieve so little. The way out is to recognise that our failure to break through has nothing to do with barriers and bias, but is explained by the fact that our society is already remarkably open to those with talent. In a relatively meritocratic country where family life is still valued, there are limits to how much more open things can be made. Far from expanding its remit, the Social Mobility Commission should pack up its bags and go home.

---

stupid? Is it possible (or fair) to stop high-income parents from making the same choices as poorer ones (one can imagine a black market in screening developing if the law is used to stop some parents taking advantage of this technology)? What desirable characteristics might get screened out of the gene pool by selecting embryos for, say, high IQ SNPs? And if widespread screening succeeded in raising IQ levels, wouldn't this mean intelligent people would in future have to be recruited to perform necessary, low-skill jobs which they would find deeply unsatisfying?

Social mobility stories

There is a legitimate discussion to be had about whether we want to live in a meritocracy. This, of course, was the question posed by Michael Young in his dystopian novel that kicked this whole debate off back in 1958, and it has two principal aspects to it.

One is the social aspect, which is that meritocracies are not egalitarian societies. Rather, they stratify the population into what Herrnstein and Murray call 'cognitive classes', and although there is still considerable movement between these classes (for intelligent parents do not always have bright children, and some intelligent kids get born into the lower strata in every generation and then move upwards), it does seem that they are becoming more distinct and polarised as modern technologies put an increasing premium on talent.[311]

Those Murray calls the 'new upper class' – the cognitively privileged – command increasingly high salaries. They attend the same universities, they marry each other, they get good jobs in the professions or top management, and they live in expensive, exclusive neighbourhoods in parts of London, the south east and the university towns where they cultivate a distinctive culture and lifestyle. They share

---

[311] Richard Herrnstein and Charles Murray, *The Bell Curve*, op cit. Also Charles Murray, *Coming Apart*, Crown Forum, 2012

a sense of entitlement (just as Young feared they would), and they have become increasingly detached from (and dismissive of) those Murray calls the 'new lower class.'

This lower cognitive class consists of people with relatively little education whose labour is less-and-less valued in a high-technology world. At the extremes, their lives are often blighted by long spells of welfare dependency coupled with criminality and family breakdown. In Britain, they can often be found corralled onto council estates.

Michael Young's novel, it will be remembered, culminates in an uprising of the socially-excluded masses against an aloof, privileged cognitive elite. There are clear signs that precisely this division has been sharpening in real-life, meritocratic Britain, although the likelihood of the lower cognitive class successfully challenging the hegemony of the higher cognitive class seems remote (as I write, the latter won't even allow a popular referendum result with which they disagree to be implemented).

And then there is the moral question about meritocracy (which Young also identified in his novel). Why should people be rewarded for talents and personality traits they have done nothing to deserve? It's not just cognitive ability that is at issue here, for we have seen that effort, too, may to a large extent be the product of our DNA. We might feel it is right that hard-working people should be rewarded for their efforts, but according to Plomin, individuals can't help being born diligent or lazy, any more than they can help being born bright or dim.

Our genes are not our destiny (even naturally lazy people can choose to make a greater effort – it's just more difficult for them). But the DNA we inherit from our parents does seem to play a very large part in shaping the kinds of people we are, and hence our prospects for success in life. Does this weaken the ethical case for rewarding both effort and ability?[312]

These are the crunchy issues about meritocracy that our politicians should be debating. But whatever conclusions we come to about the desirability of meritocracy, it is impossible to have any sensible debate at all until we acknowledge the evidence showing just how meritocratic we already are.

We do not live in a *perfect* meritocracy, and it is inconceivable that we ever will. Unless and until the Marxist left fulfils its age-old dream of abolishing the family, there will never be a perfectly level playing field on which all children can compete. Some parents will always encourage their children more than others do – help them learn to read, boost their confidence, push them to stretch themselves to the limits of their talent. Some parents will always be more able or willing than others to give their kids a bit of help when they need it – to look after their grandchildren so their daughter can return to her full-time career, or to offer a deposit so their son can afford to buy a flat near his dream job in London. Children will continue to follow their parents into the family business, whether it is selling groceries in a corner shop or farming a few hundred acres of land, and they will always grow up influenced by different parental role models. Where one child hears talk

---

[312] In *The Son Also Rises*, Gregory Clark argues that if social mobility is driven by innate characteristics rooted in our genes, we should stop worrying about promoting 'opportunity' and removing 'obstacles', and should instead focus on narrowing the reward differentials between successful and unsuccessful people. More recently, Daniel Markovits's book, *The Meritocracy Trap* (Penguin, 2019), has similarly made a strong case against the very principle of 'just desserts'. However, if we start to move away from the meritocratic ideal of rewarding those who work hard and put their talents to good use, we shall rapidly end up indulging idleness and discouraging effort, and that way lies cultural decadence and economic ruin. I discuss this issue in more depth in *Social Mobility Myths* where I relate it to the long-forgotten sociological debate in the 1950s about the positive 'functionality' of social stratification.

of the law over the dinner table every evening, and almost 'automatically' gravitates towards a legal career, another grows up never thinking about the law and perhaps never seriously considers it as a career. These things are not going to change much, whatever politicians do.[313]

In this sense, we do not all start out 'equal', and we never can. But we have also seen that parenting does not have much impact on most children's social class destinations. A bright girl born to doctor parents is quite likely to become a doctor herself – but she would almost certainly have ended up in some equivalent middle class career whatever her parentage. Meanwhile, her less intellectually-gifted brother will struggle to emulate his parents' status, no matter how much they spend on his school fees.

'Equality of opportunity' requires that any obstacles placed in the path of those from more humble origins should be removed – and in the last 75 years in Britain, for the most part, they have been. Today, if you have the ability and the desire, there is nothing to stop you from achieving your ambition. This is what a 'warts and all' meritocracy looks like. It is what most of our politicians keep telling us they want to achieve, yet we already have it.

---

[313] Oddly, perhaps, John Goldthorpe has ended up in his latest book largely agreeing with this. Recognising that parents will always try to support their children in whatever ways they can (culturally, as well as financially), he suggests that perfect fluidity is probably unobtainable, and certainly lies 'beyond political reach.' He goes on: 'Parents who read their children bedtime stories or engage with them in "supper table debates" give them clear developmental advantages. But to prevent parents from doing these things would neither be feasible nor in any event desirable. The crucial fact that has to be faced is that many activities that could be regarded as *constitutive of family life* serve in themselves to create significant inequalities of opportunity among children from their early years onwards... some degree of inequality in relative mobility chances... has to be accepted as an integral and persisting feature of British society: that is, as following directly from the existence of the institution [of the family], which may, of course, on other grounds be valued' (*Social mobility and education in Britain*, p.221-2).

The truth is, what many social mobility campaigners today are really interested in achieving is not meritocracy (equal opportunity) but equality of outcomes. They complain about 'too many' middle class students in Oxbridge or 'not enough' working class lawyers, but they pay little or no regard to the ability and effort displayed by those who currently achieve these positions. For them, the only acceptable measure of a 'fair' system is that every social group in the population should be equally represented in every social position. To achieve this, they demand, not just that obstacles be removed from the path of the least advantaged, but that new obstacles be created and deliberately placed in the paths of those born into more advantageous family circumstances. We live in an age of creeping class targets and quotas.

Such policies have nothing to do with achieving meritocracy or 'fairness.' Indeed, they subvert it. Forcing universities to vary their entrance criteria according to the social class of the applicant, or badgering employers into taking on more applicants from particular kinds of backgrounds in order to fulfil their social class quotas – these are the antithesis of the 'meritocracy' that campaigners claim they want to achieve. Policies like these are not warranted by the evidence. They are not even necessary. And they are certainly not 'just.'

I began my earlier essay, *Social Mobility Myths*, with the story of my father, Albert Saunders, who was born into a working class family in Croydon in 1925. I make no apology for ending this one by repeating it, for there are lessons in Albert's story that the current generation of politicians have forgotten.

Albert did not pass the Scholarship examination at age eleven, so he went to the local Elementary School. His father, a painter and decorator with the London County Council, knew little of education and offered him no encouragement, but Albert was diligent and well-behaved, and when the time came for him to leave school, his class teacher found him a job as a shop assistant at a men's outfitters. His father overruled this, however, telling his son that he should not get ideas above his station. Blue-collar work had been good enough for him all his life and it should be good enough for Albert too. So it was that, in the Spring of 1939, just after he turned 14, my father started work as a machine operative in a local factory.

On the day he left school, he asked his class teacher to sign his autograph book. That teacher wrote in his book:

Aim high,
For though you may not reach the sky,
You will most certainly reach the mountain tops.

As soon as he was old enough, Albert joined the RAF where he eventually earned his wings as a bomber pilot. After the war he applied for teacher training and started teaching P.E. in one of the new Secondary Modern schools. Later in life he taught in schools in Zambia and Uganda, trained miners in Namibia in basic literacy and numeracy, and in his fifties won a place at university back in Britain to study for a Bachelor of Education degree. Today, at the age of 94, he still speaks fondly of that form teacher who inspired him at his Elementary School.

The message that teacher wrote in my father's autograph book was a message of hope and aspiration. It spoke of opportunity, not despair; of ambition, not fatalism. This is the opposite of the message that children from humble backgrounds are being given in today's Britain. All they hear from the media and their country's political leaders today is how badly the odds are stacked against them – how children like them are unlikely to succeed no matter how hard they try; how they live in a rigidly class stratified society which looks after the kids from affluent homes but keeps kids like them out of the best schools, the best universities and the best jobs.

None of it is true, but the obvious danger is that this relentlessly depressing and pessimistic stream of ill-informed propaganda becomes a self-fulfilling prophecy. If you're young, and you get told often enough that your chances of succeeding in life are slim, it's no surprise if eventually you just give up trying. What's the point in struggling with algebra, German grammar and the mystery of the periodic table if none of it is going to lead you anywhere?

The bitter irony is that the message these kids are being fed is completely false. The chances of bright, hard-working children from working class homes succeeding in the education system and ending up in high-status, well-paid, responsible jobs are extremely good. In today's Britain, talent and hard work easily trump social class background. The system is much more meritocratic than we are commonly led to believe. We should be telling our children this, rather than filling their heads with Marxist fairy tales about unfair privilege and class bias. Maybe then, more of them will go on to fulfil their potential in the future, just as Albert (and millions of other working class kids like him) managed to do in the past.